NOW

THAT I HAVE YOUR ATTENTION

NOW

THAT I HAVE YOUR ATTENTION

7 LESSONS IN LEADING A LIFE BIGGER THAN THEY EXPECT

NICOLAS HAMILTON

RADAR

First published in Great Britain in 2024 by Radar,
an imprint of Octopus Publishing Group Ltd
Carmelite House
50 Victoria Embankment
London EC4Y 0DZ
www.octopusbooks.co.uk

An Hachette UK Company
www.hachette.co.uk

ISBN (Hardback) 978-1-80419-170-5
ISBN (Trade paperback) 978-1-80419-171-2

A CIP catalogue record for this book is available from the British Library.

Typeset in 12/17.5pt Sabon LT Pro by Jouve (UK), Milton Keynes

Printed and bound in Great Britain

1 3 5 7 9 10 8 6 4 2

This FSC® label means that materials used for
the product have been responsibly sourced.

MIX
Paper | Supporting responsible forestry
FSC® C104740
FSC www.fsc.org

For my Mumma & Pops and anyone who is scared to take 'the leap', you CAN do it!

CONTENTS

AUTHOR'S NOTE

In crafting this book, I am acutely aware of the complex nature of the experiences I share. It is my sincerest intention to convey my personal journey without casting judgement on the paths of others. This book is not an endorsement of a 'tragedy narrative'; rather, it seeks to illuminate the triumphs and challenges that have shaped my life.

As a proud advocate for the disabled community, I firstly want to acknowledge the importance of mobility aids in the lives of many, and I am aware of the potential alienation my descriptions may evoke. It is not my intention to diminish the significance of these devices; rather, I hope to offer insight into my own evolution and perspectives. I recognize that for some, mobility aids represent liberation, and I honour that perspective.

In recounting my experiences, I aim to provide a lens into the intricacies of personal growth and the ways in which I navigated the world. I do not seek to diminish the structural barriers that exist, but rather, emphasize the power of the individual to forge their own path.

I also wish to say that language is a powerful tool and I have endeavoured to use it thoughtfully. I understand the importance of terminology in the disability community and have striven to strike a balance that respects the preferences of diverse voices. My sincerest hope is that I walk this line with care, but I can't say I am perfect on this front.

This book is an exploration of my journey, my triumphs, my tribulations and my evolving perspectives. It is not a prescriptive guide for all, but rather an invitation to reflect on the diverse narratives that shape our lives. I extend my deepest gratitude to you, the reader, for joining me on this journey.

With warm regards,
Nicolas Hamilton

INTRODUCTION

For the majority of my life, I felt as if my voice didn't matter. Growing up, it felt like no one had the time to listen to my thoughts or opinions, and that nothing I said or thought mattered to anyone. No one ever asked what was up with me. No one ever said are you OK?, or if they did it didn't feel like they really cared about the answer. I remember feeling so frustrated, but at the time I just couldn't put that frustration into words.

Of course, that wasn't the only thing that bothered me because my situation had more challenges than most. At home, my dad and older brother Lewis were busy building extraordinary careers within motorsport and that meant our whole family's focus was on supporting that. At the same time, Mum was trying to hold it all together, which was far from easy. You see, I was born two months premature with a condition which completely upended my family's life. During my birth the left side of my brain was starved of oxygen, which led to the development of spastic diplegia, a form of cerebral palsy (CP) which affects the lower half of my body. As my condition is neurological and permanently affects my muscles and coordination, my parents were given a pretty sobering prognosis when I was just 18 months old: I might never be able to walk, and if I did, it would be, *at best*, with a stick or some sort of aid. More than likely, I would need to use a wheelchair for most of my life, which would make living independently very difficult. It was a crushing moment for them and for the whole family. Physically, I required an enormous amount of support and help, which was a huge responsibility for mostly my mum to shoulder.

When you're disabled, you become aware of your position in society from a very young age. The spaces and places you are excluded from because of your abilities, the activities you just can't join in with, the stares and attention you receive from other children and adults alike mark you out. Added to that, I was also the only mixed-race kid at any of my schools, which made me even more of a sore thumb. Back then, we weren't well off at all, and my parents were really limited as to the kind of support and resources they could fund for me. Initially, Mum, Dad, Lewis and I were living in a one-bedroom flat, and times were really tough. There is only so much you can do to protect any child from the truth of the world and before I even made it to reception class at school, I knew I was on the back foot. Coming to understand my position in the world when I was young was really depressing, and I soon realized that, no matter how much my parents might want to help, I was very much alone.

My parents decided early on that they weren't going to let my prognosis dictate my destiny, so I was sent to mainstream nursery and schools throughout my childhood. In many ways that was wonderful, but there were also a lot of hard lessons to be learned, and during those years it felt again like my voice was drowned out.

Over the first weeks and months at school, no one spoke to me or wanted to be my friend and I was treated like a freak, a dweeb, someone you would gawp at rather than hang out with. I was the opposite of cool. Although the teachers showed interest and provided help for my schooling, they struggled to connect with me. Of course, they were overworked and overstretched and had 30 able-bodied kids to manage too, but those experiences made me feel incredibly small and insignificant. Back then, I would have been grateful for someone even taking the time to argue with me, because at least it would have meant that they had heard my voice, that they had listened and acknowledged that I was there. I spent so long as a young person just feeling completely invisible.

Being ignored by my peers, by nearly everyone around me, shaped much of my young life, making me feel rejected and worthless. I know many teenagers feel exactly the same, whether they are navigating special requirements or not. It's probably why so many of us rush to grow up. On top of that feeling of being tiny, at school I heard other messages – 'He's never going anywhere', 'He won't amount to anything' – from kids and teachers alike. Then the doctors and the endless number of people who spoke *about* me and not *to* me. 'It's never going to work out for him.' Feeling dismissed by adults and having this sense that I wasn't acknowledged in the room when people were talking about me had a really awful impact on my sense of identity. When you believe that your voice has no value, you stop speaking. I felt no one understood or would ever understand anything about me, so I learned to keep my feelings inside.

Today, every year, tens of thousands of people *now* listen to what I have to say. I have built a career around my voice and have used it to change not just my life but other people's too. The journey has been *a ride* and there have been both extraordinary lows and extraordinary highs along the way. I have defied all the odds, using the power of mentality to push myself physically beyond all expectations. Today I walk entirely unaided and live an independent life in my own house. After building myself up physically, I decided to follow my dreams and break down so many barriers to become the first ever disabled racing driver to compete in the Renault Clio Cup, the European Touring Car Cup and the British Touring Car Championship (BTCC), known as the pinnacle of British motorsport. I continue to compete against able-bodied drivers and in 2023 I achieved a personal best sixth place result in a BTCC race, further cementing my name in the history books, raising the bar to inspire more disabled drivers. On top of this, I have simultaneously created an incredibly successful career as a motivational speaker, travelling to share my voice and story across the globe.

But inevitably, there have also been many unbelievable failures, setbacks and catastrophes which have, at times, shaken me to my core. I've had days when I preferred to be asleep than awake and I've lived through weeks of suicidal thoughts. So many things that have happened to me – some I've been responsible for and others which have just been terrible luck – could have derailed me for good. There has been so much distress and darkness, but I have always managed to find my way back to the light. In this book, through a series of lessons based on moments of intense struggle, unexpected achievements and crossroads in my life, I want to show you exactly how I came back from rock bottom to create a life with deep foundations. I truly want these lessons to bring hope to people who are in the trenches and provide a blueprint for anyone who is anywhere near as lost as I was.

I'm not saying the way I do things is the only way, or the right way. Not at all. This is just the way that worked for me, and that doesn't mean it will work for everyone, though I think that there will be something that will resonate for most of you somewhere in my words. My real aim in this book is simply to lay it all out frankly and show that impossible things can be done. This story is really about how I went from being born with a life-altering condition and told that I might never walk, to being a disabled man who travels the world independently and has overcome pretty much every barrier put in front of him, as well as earning money, building a career and finding a place in society. You might have wondered how a man like me could have possibly transformed from the boy who felt he had nothing to offer anyone. How did I go from that little lad with a walking frame to a man who drives racing cars at 150mph? I want to put everything I have learned on the record, just in case it helps anyone else. If you pick up the book and it supports you, great! If you pick it up and it upsets you, that was absolutely not the intention, but equally I can't please everyone. All I can do is be transparent and recount my journey as accurately as possible. My goal is to be honest and open and if you can take something from it, that is an incredible bonus.

I have felt at times unworthy of writing a book, that no one would ever be interested in my life. I'm nothing special, or different or better than the next person. Everyone has a story and everybody goes through difficult things, right? Often, we experience things that are broadly similar, just in slightly different ways. So, I never really saw myself as notable, even when people I respected were encouraging me to put my story down on paper. I always felt like the people who deserved to write books were those who had completed their rags-to-riches story, celebrities who had achieved a great deal and had a lot of impact. They are the people that others want to hear about, people like my brother. And that isn't me. I believed my voice wasn't exceptional enough. I suppose I was also – *I am* – nervous about putting myself out there and making it seem as though I rate myself as something special. I like to think I'm a modest man, and writing a book about yourself isn't exactly modest, is it? But over time my mentality has shifted and now I know that what I have to share isn't really about me, because the power some of these stories have to help others goes way beyond my reservations. As a good friend said to me, it was time to get over myself.

I truly believe that everyone can relate to something written on these pages. My disability is part of the story, but it's not the main character and many of the things I've been through are universal struggles, things that nearly everyone has touched, gone through or will go through at some point in their life. I know how many of us have been taught to shroud some of these battles in silence and shame, that some of the things I now stand up and speak about on stage are stories which many of you might feel unable to share with your closest friends and family. I couldn't empathize more, because I have been there. But savage honesty is really the only route out and forwards, and I hope you can all take comfort from seeing me talk about these issues completely without shame. My aim is that this acts like a domino and helps you knock over your own dominos of pride or embarrassment or discomfort so you too can face your demons head-on.

When it comes to my stories around disability, my God, I wish this book had existed when I was a teenager grappling with these totally uncharted waters with a head full of questions that no one knew the answers to. Equally, my mum, who has also contributed to this book, has admitted how much something like this would have helped her too. Being a parent to a disabled child can be a really lonely path and it goes without saying that being disabled can be an incredibly isolating existence too. One of my biggest goals is to provide a voice to those people who feel left out by the rest of society. My world of motorsport is still a really niche industry and I want my story to reach people far outside of my fan base, or even my brother's massive fan base. I want this book to reach a 16-year-old boy who might be battling with his disability while also wanting to have relationships. As a disabled person, you can feel that so many of the joys of life aren't available to you, but I want to say to anyone who feels excluded and lost in life – disabled or not – and doesn't believe there is any way they will ever find their place or be happy, that it's just not true. I want the book to get into the hands of people at rock bottom, people in the midst of depression or addiction who can't see a way out. I also want parents who are struggling to guide their children to read it and see ways they can help. Or any family who loves a child born on the back foot, no matter how that manifests itself – physically, mentally, materially or through a lack of privilege.

This book is an account of how you can travel from A to B. Your start lines and finish lines will look different from mine and our paths might be incomparable. But I just want to let people know there *is* a course between the two points. You are the only person who can prove your own potential – you can't find it on a graph or in a list of data or statistics or held within anyone else's expectations. There is a path for everyone which can end in relative success. That success can never be judged in comparison to anyone else's: each of us only competes against ourselves, because we can only stretch as far as we go. I am never going to be a seven-times Formula 1 World Champion like my big brother, but that doesn't mean that I haven't fulfilled my potential any less. Success can be walking up three steps without holding onto anything for support – something which I can say because I know what an incredible achievement it was to me as a child. Success can look tiny to someone else but be immense to you. Success is truly in the eye of the beholder.

Nowadays my voice attracts attention and is heard beyond my family and even beyond my sport. Sometimes I do think, what changed? When was the moment that I became deserving of other people's attention? After all those years of being written off and being told I had nothing to bring to the table, *now* I'm worth listening to? It's hard not to wonder where people were when I was totally on my arse. I want anyone who feels passed over or unworthy of attention to really hear this: you are valuable today. You are valuable tomorrow. You don't need to change a single thing about yourself to be worthy. Your voice means something no matter what you do or who you are. I am no more full of worth as a person than I was when I was overlooked by the world, just because I have managed to achieve some things and tick some boxes. My voice always mattered and so does yours.

Some of the stories I'm sharing here feel gut-wrenchingly painful. I'm not a fool, I know that there may be some not-so-lovely feedback coming my way. I know what it feels like to be hung out to dry in a public arena and sharing my story with the world inevitably means dealing with the press and brutal elements of social media commentary, something which has been part of my life for a long time now. When it comes down to it, I've learned to live with a lot of it, but of course there are things that I am nervous about. If I was just an anonymous dude living his own life and all the characters in my story were completely unknown, I would be relaxed about putting my experiences out into the world. I'm not ashamed of who I am or what I've done because it all got me to where I am today. But when you are part of a family in the public eye, there is a lot at stake. I know that anything I say or do has the potential to reflect either poorly or positively on Lewis and to a lesser extent my dad, and I love and respect them both deeply, so I have done my best to navigate that. I also know that people will see what they want to and that, for some, tearing other people down and judging them helps make them feel better or more secure about themselves. I do have visions of awful headlines which won't read 'Nic Hamilton did X', but instead will say 'Lewis Hamilton's brother did X'. It's so sad that it has to be that way.

None of the bad times is my family's fault and many of my achievements and the good times I've enjoyed are down to the positive influence that they've had on my life. It wasn't their fault that I was born with this condition, and everyone has done their very best for me, to the very best of their abilities. No one expects or is taught how to manage these often very complicated issues.

I just hope that you can read through my lessons with an open mind and an open heart, with empathy and generosity for everyone involved. It can make a person feel so incredibly detached from the rest of the world when they look around and see everyone else on this obvious, successful path. While I'm not saying I'm a role model for anything, I do believe we all need more role models who give you the full 360-degree story and don't miss out the gnarly bits. At the end of the day, this is my book, my life and my story. I take full responsibility for every single one of my mistakes, of which there are many and varied. Like any grumpy teenager, there were moments when I might have resented my parents, but when it all comes out in the wash, I feel so blessed that I came into the world as their son.

My family knows the power of my story and what a difference my honesty could make to difficult conversations. Conversations around sex and money and depression and addiction and countless other topics that can be very painful to address.

As for how some of my messages will be appraised by the world, we live in such polarized times, it's sometimes hard to work out how you can speak on any topic without offending loudly. I feel like my philosophy really spans generations and politics. It's a little bit boomer in some places, a little bit 'woke' in others. I hope that can show people that there are multiple ways to think about everything. My attitude is really a mix of lots of ideas and I've chosen them to make my own bespoke mantras. I'm very emotionally open and believe deeply in working on yourself. I also believe that traumas have long-lasting impact and that showing your vulnerability is a strength – my heart is entirely on my sleeve. There are people out there who might say this is snowflake talk. Move on, mate. Equally,

I do preach and practise a level of 'pull your socks up': if you physically can do something, I always believe you should try to do it. Self-reliance is ingrained in me.

I can often come from a place of individualism. One side of the way I see the world and its challenges comes from my dad, and some people out there will feel it is quite harsh. If you boil everything he has taught me down, I think it's basically that life *is* what it is. Stop moaning about things you can't change; instead, get on with it and get through as much as you can. For me personally, this was incredibly useful in helping me overcome things that I was told were insurmountable, but at a certain point I needed some balance to keep me mentally able to continue along that positive path. I had to admit that, on certain days and at certain times, I struggled to 'just do it'. Maybe I wanted to cry, maybe I needed to let it all out. And by showing my vulnerability and being kind to myself in those moments, I've actually made myself stronger in the long run. The end result is better for me this way. So, I've managed to take what my dad has instilled in me, which I am so grateful for – drive, passion, grit, determination – and blend that with empathy for myself and the acknowledgement that it's OK to struggle and notice that you're struggling.

I don't want to tell you how to read this book or how it should be used. I have found reading a challenge for my whole life and want to admit here that I'm definitely not a bookworm. It sounds silly to say, but reading both out loud and in my head has totally overwhelmed me in the past, which was why it was so important for me to record an audio version too. I also don't want to tell you how it should make you feel or what it should encourage you to do.

Across these pages I offer all kinds of advice, most of it learned through sometimes harrowing real-life experience. I would love to say that I always take the high road and make all the right choices, but I don't. Even today, I'm a work in progress and as you go through these chapters there may be moments where you think, 'Nic! No! How could you have done that?' While I might be here dishing it all out, I want to be very clear that I'm not some model human. I have become a better human through my trials and tribulations, but like everyone else, there is still a lot for me to figure out. I've ignored lots of well-meaning advice over the years, sometimes for the better, but often for the worse. We all need to make our own mistakes, crash out of the race, fall off the rails. You learn very little solely from success except for how much better it feels in comparison to fucking up. So here we go, time to strap in, let's go.

Before I go any further, I want to write a personal message to my family. My mum Linda, my dad Anthony and my brother Lewis: they are my three heroes. Everything you read in this book, no matter how difficult some of it will be for all of you, is me saying, 'Thank you.' Thank you for being the incredible people you are. For the endless support you have shown, the sacrifices you have made, the dedication you have given to my disability and condition, the opportunities you have created for me, the lessons you have taught me and the love you have shown. I would not be the man I am today without you all. You are about to read *my* book for crying out loud. Nic's book, Pic-Nic's book, Goof's book, or even Mum's Chicken & Ham Pie's book! Whatever you read in these pages ahead, however it makes you feel – joyful, happy, sad, frustrated or whatever – it is me saying 'Thank you' for absolutely everything.

I wouldn't have changed any of it for the world. I am so proud to be your son and your brother and I hope that I have made you all proud too.

I love you all more than you will ever know.

Nic x

To everyone else, thank you for wanting to listen to me.

Now that I have your attention, I hope to inspire you.

LESSON ONE

REBEL AGAINST THE RULEBOOK

Let's start with the frustrating truth: no matter who you are, other people are going to put you in a box. The problem this presents to each and every one of us is that those people's expectations of how you will live and how you will behave can derail your dreams and lead you on a path to a smaller life. Their pre-disposed ideas can even go so far as to stop you from daring to dream you can achieve certain things. This shit can totally shape your time on Earth and reduce your potential to experience literally countless joys. If you're told something isn't possible, it takes a massive leap of faith to push against that. If you are told *enough times,* by *enough people*, that something isn't possible, it takes something even more: defiance. In this chapter, I hope I can inspire you to tune out the noise and truly take on board the fact that many of the limits we believe are set in stone are actually imaginary. Yes, the hurdles and obstacles you have to overcome in order to get to where you want to be can be brutal. Yes, you are going to have to be hardcore with your work ethic and learn to pick yourself up from the ground time and time again. No one is offering anything on a plate here. You're also going to have to learn to believe in yourself, which, as I know from my own experience, is probably the hardest piece of the puzzle.

As a disabled mixed-race man, exclusion is something I have to deal with on a daily basis, and it is absolutely right that we confront the excessive unfair barriers that people face. But I am also very much a believer in the power inside each of us to define our own destinies and, as corny as that sounds, I wanted to open this book by having a frank conversation around what it takes to turn expectations on their head, no matter what your situation or position on this planet. In my life there have been *so* many times when I would have been excluded if I had let other people's ideas define what I am capable of. I would never, *ever* have achieved a fraction of what I have in life if I had listened to what other people saw as my upper limits. But what are often labelled 'insurmountable hurdles' *can* be overcome. Just because no one has done something before, it doesn't mean you can't be the first, and just because other people think you can't do something doesn't mean you have to listen. I am living, walking proof of that. What it does require, however, is a bit of stubborn rebellion and a willingness to push against the grain, which isn't exactly what you're taught at school.

As for being a rebel, I believe my tendency to ignore 'advice and guidance' from pretty much everyone – including my family from time to time – has been fundamental to my success. Rebelling against almost everything that I was told has led to really positive outcomes. For some reason, the concept of being an outlier, or someone who doesn't conform, is still viewed as a negative in many scenarios in life. At school, for example, you are so strongly encouraged to fit the mould and follow the 'usual' path, and that message bleeds into our young lives so that we can often feel that only certain routes are open to us. I really want to instil in you how important it is to think for yourself and make up your own mind about what it is you actually want. I'm not saying you have to spend your life in detention as a kid or grow up to be this wild disruptor of every industry. Your personal rebellion might be quieter and far less radical. But out of the many, many things in life that you can't change, questioning whether to follow the path, be it staying in school to do your A-levels or doing a certain job, or rebelling to start building your career in an industry that perhaps your parents don't approve of, is one thing that you can master.

PUSHING BACK AGAINST EXCLUSION: BEHIND THE WHEEL

When I was 18, I decided that I wanted to break into motorsport. Now this was, in many ways, absurd. To my knowledge, there had never been a physically disabled driver in British motorsport. In order to effectively use the brakes in the car I would have to drive, I'd need to be able to push 70kg worth of pressure with my left leg, when at that point I could only manage about 10kg with both. Every other driver in the field was not only able-bodied, they had been competing since they were children, working their way up the motorsport ladder, starting with go-karts from around the age of eight. I had no credentials or practical know-how. Motorsport is also insanely expensive. Oh, and I only had two months from deciding I wanted to compete to prepare for my first race. There's unlikely and then there's this kind of challenge.

But as a kid I had *always* wanted to race. My dad actually put me into a go-kart when I was seven years old and we went to a car park to learn the basics. Back then, my legs were incredibly weak. Even though I had been learning to climb stairs and walking with my frame, my muscles just weren't strong enough to use the pedals, so I inevitably crashed. The whole thing ended up being extremely dramatic, as I managed to hit a curb and disappeared down a six-foot drop, landing in inches of water. My parents literally watched me fly into the air and disappear. Just terrible! After that experience, that was always the story – no racing for Nic, because remember what happened at that car park. My dad was adamant about it, probably haunted by memories of me in that watery ditch.

However, by the time I was 18, some things had changed. I had worked to overcome some of my physical limitations and I no longer used a wheelchair. In that process, I had also bolstered my mental strength and realized the power of determination to strive for what I *actually* wanted.

For me that was to race. I had grown up in a world defined by motorsport. I was literally raised on the circuit alongside all the other drivers' brothers and sisters. Our childhoods were spent travelling between races, holed up in each other's camper vans, sharing lunches and playing games while our siblings were out on track, racing. Then it was award evenings and formal dinners wearing suits and ties, where we would have to talk to the high-ups in motorsport and be on our best behaviour. Most of us were old beyond our years, because we were around so many adults even as young kids. With both my brother and dad working in the sport, it felt very much like it was our family business and in my heart of hearts I felt it was in my blood too. But, because of my disability, any dreams of racing just seemed like a fantasy, so I had started to consider following my dad into some area of management or the business side of motorsport.

While I had a traditional state secondary-school education, all that travelling to races meant I was away *a lot*. I wasn't the most academic student, but my dad really wanted me to do well – at least better than him and Lewis – so I did work and apply myself, though it was mostly to get him off my back. I ended up getting decent grades in my GCSEs, but school just didn't fire me up. Being out of the classroom so often probably didn't help. I remember sitting my business GCSE exam and having to leave on the dot to get to the next Formula 1 race. It was like I was never fully engaged and present when I was there. When I started my A-levels I remember saying to myself, right, this time it's going to be different, I'm not going to miss weeks of school. But, before I knew it, my attendance had plummeted again, so I ended up leaving after my first year of A-levels and my school agreed it was probably for the best.

Of course, there was no way my dad was going to be leaving me to twiddle my thumbs at home. After a couple of weeks of me watching *Homes Under the Hammer* and playing computer games till 4am, he was like, 'Nic, for God's sake, get a job!' I remember sitting at the kitchen table and just thinking, what do I know about? What am I interested in? At 17, with no A-levels or degree, what on earth have I got to offer? I was struggling deeply with my feelings of self-worth as I grappled with the realities of my disability and my place in the world. I needed to prove that I had something valuable to offer and I just kept drawing a blank. It can be incredibly hard for a young person without higher education to prove to anyone that they are worth taking a chance on or that their ideas matter.

At the time, the only value I could come up with was my experience and understanding of motorsport and gaming. I'd been playing simulation racing games for years now and I actually became a UK champion in one game, marking the culmination of many years of practice and dedication. It all started when I received a 'demo' of a game called GTR through the door. It was 2005, I was 13 and back then game stores would send demos of new releases to your house as a marketing strategy. I remember taking this particular game upstairs to my room, plugging in my gamepad (controller) and going for it. That was my first experience of a simulation game and one that I became almost immediately addicted to. I bought a cheap steering wheel and pedals from PC World and spent all of my time practising. At the time, I was still at school and using a wheelchair, so my legs weren't strong enough or fast enough to use the pedals, and this meant I had to develop a technique of using the buttons on the steering wheel as my accelerator and brake. This was a disadvantage because, as with motorsport, throttle and brake modulation is vital to controlling the car and car balance into and out of corners. The buttons on my steering wheel were either 100 per cent throttle or brake or 0 per cent, with no in-between, so I had to adapt to a whole new driving style.

One day, I was driving a simulated Ferrari 550 around the historic Monza circuit and Lewis came into my room while I was setting a lap time. Straightaway, he said, 'Good lap, now let me beat it!'

He could see that I wasn't using pedals, so to keep it fair he just used the buttons on the steering wheel too. That day, when I left the house to go to school, Lewis spent the day trying to beat my lap time. When I returned, he was really excited that after all his hours of hard work, he'd bested me. I remember keeping my cool and being like, 'OK, OK, no worries, my turn.' It took me two laps and I beat his time again, with Lewis screaming 'No waaaaay!' in the background. A story, and some brotherly competitiveness, that neither of us will ever forget.

As the years went on, new versions of this particular game were released, along with other games by the same developer, SimBin Studios, which I collected and played. I came across communities which held professional championships and online races on the newest game, RACE 07. It was now 2009 and I was very experienced, so I decided to enter the British Championship through the official community and ended up winning, using buttons on a £20 steering wheel, racing against able-bodied drivers with much more hi-spec equipment. It was a massive moment for me.

After my success in simulation racing, it was like a switch had been turned on and my mentality began to shift. At the same time, getting out of my wheelchair – which I'll tell you more about later – had sparked a little bit of hope inside me and made me begin to dream again. If I could achieve this, what else was out there for me?

Lewis and I played racing games a lot over the years – it has always been a great way for us to spend time together. Over time, he started to comment that I seemed to have a sort of talent for and understanding of racing and driving; then one day he said, 'I know you have always wanted to – don't you think it's time you gave it a go for real?' I sat on it for a while before approaching my dad, because I knew he wasn't going to be keen. It was going to be, 'Remember what happened when you were seven!' But when I did decide to speak with him, very calmly, I told him that I was a man now. I had already overcome so much in my life, and I felt I was finally in a position where things might go differently.

The conversation, perhaps predictably, didn't immediately go my way. Dad listed all the barriers and problems ahead; some of them he felt were insurmountable. But I used the mentality that he had instilled in me to remind him of all the ways that impossible was a construct. I reminded him of the many, many ways our family had already overcome things which we had been told were impossible. I reminded him that I didn't need my wheelchair – and could walk now – something that we had been told was impossible. Basically, I went for the jugular and didn't give up. I was rebelling against the rulebook. In the end, he said he had run out of excuses. He finally agreed to give me a chance, as I believe that he wouldn't have been able to live with himself if he didn't let me try. Don't get me wrong, I believe he thought I was going to fail, but for him to give me the opportunity, regardless of his thoughts, was a powerful gift for any parent to give to their child. He called the owner of this driving school we knew and arranged the day. I don't know what he actually said, he probably told him that I might struggle, but he wanted to give me this chance. He probably told him about the car park incident too, who knows? But none of that mattered to me because I knew how fortunate I was to even get a shot. I felt absolutely euphoric – finally I was going to get to be a part of something that I'd been watching from the sidelines my entire life.

The driving-school owner put me in a BMW M3, and it was the first time I'd ever driven any car of race pedigree. I'd got my road driving licence at 17, passing first time – I don't need modifications to a road car, and drive a standard automatic – but driving a car like that was obviously a very different experience. On that first outing, I drove with the chief instructor and by the end of the day I had matched his lap time. That probably sounds like I'm exaggerating, but I'm not – I just had this innate understanding of how to drive cars. It felt intuitive and completely natural, as if this was what I was meant to be doing with my life.

When we got home, I couldn't believe the day I'd had. All I wanted to do was get back out there again. But before the conversation could go any further, a week or so later Dad took me back to the track, just to make sure it wasn't beginner's luck, and I managed to replicate the same lap time. I remember Dad taking this long, deep breath. My parents were wary of going through the whole racing experience again. They didn't know if they could put another son through the intense expectations of racing and obviously, with me being disabled as well, it was going to add another unknown layer to the whole impossible thing. But after that second day Dad said, 'If you want to race, then you have to work hard', which was his version of, 'Go for it, but it's not going to be easy.'

Usually, as an aspiring young driver, you would start your journey into the sport right at the bottom in go-karts, work your way up into cars and end up where I am today. Or else you'd go down the single-seater route with the aim of ending up in Formula 1. Dad's plan was for me to do the Renault Clio Cup Championship, which at the time was the toughest one-make series (a racing series where everyone goes head-to-head in the exact same car) in the UK. It's a step below the British Touring Car Championship, which was and is the pinnacle of British motorsport, and it's highly, highly competitive. I knew I would be racing against all the touring-car protégés, aged between 16 and 25, who would have all been honing their skills since they were eight years old. Dad also said that he would help fund this first season, and help me get some sponsorship together, but as motorsport is so insanely expensive, I would have to organize my own funding going forward. I couldn't believe it was all happening, and I didn't pause to think about the future. Just dealing with the magnitude of what was happening right in that moment was enough. But once it had sunk in, I quickly thought, how the hell was I going to drive the car competitively?

In order to compete on as close to a level playing field as possible, we knew that I would need the car modified in some way. I decided that I wouldn't use hand controls and would instead work to strengthen my legs. Going straight to hand controls would have been easier, but I know from long experience that the easy way is not always the best way. So I was going to drive with modified pedals instead. This was probably the biggest mountain I had to climb in my motorsport journey. People don't understand how physical motorsport truly is. Braking is *everything* – as I learned to my detriment as that seven-year-old in the car park. Think of the effort of an emergency stop in a road car – in racing you do that every single time you hit the brake pedal, because you want to brake as late as possible to be as competitive as possible.

For two months, I basically lived at the gym. I was there constantly, sitting on the leg press and building, building, building the weight I could push with my legs. I literally could not count the number of hours I put into it, working on my legs, and it was gruelling and painful. I didn't really worry about my arms because they were already strong due to me being in the wheelchair for so long and using them for general movement on a daily basis. If I worked them even more, I'd get too big. You don't want to be bulky for the car – it's about being as strong and as lean as possible and, in my case, it's more about space and ease of movement. While I was training, I applied to the Motorsport Association (MSA) for my racing licence, which I absolutely had to have in order to be allowed to race. We heard back pretty quickly that my licence had been declined outright because I was disabled.

From the MSA's perspective, I can understand why there might have been concerns, but I truly don't believe that a blanket ban is ever fair. Anyway, with my rebel hat on, there was no way I was going to accept it. The first step to getting your licence is to complete the ARDS (Association of Racing Driver Schools) test, where you have to be able to drive a car around a track competently and hit certain braking points and turning points. If you lock a brake or spin at any point, you instantly fail. I'd already passed my ARDS test, and from that point it usually takes an able-bodied person two weeks to get their licence. For me, that story was to be different. As soon as I heard I had been turned down, I reapplied immediately, to let it be known that I wasn't just going to roll over and accept the decision. I told them I was not going to allow the motorsport industry to put me in a box and not make me feel welcome as a disabled driver and that I would continue pushing.

The MSA ended up sending their disability commissioner over to my house to assess how able I was. While the MSA was right to take every step to ensure the safety of everyone, it seemed to me they missed the mark by overlooking the needs of the individual driver. I understand that I was not your average applicant, but I was nonetheless an applicant with the desire to race. To me, if you are going to really judge the impact of a mobility issue or indeed any other ability, surely you would want to have a collection of standardized tests which are assessed by experts in their respective fields. An assessment at a 'motorsport centre', which has a gym and a physiotherapist, who is both an expert working with professionals in motorsport and is able to inspect the limitations of a condition, would at the very least seem sensible. If the MSA had said, 'Nic, if you want to be a racing driver, let our motorsport physiotherapist understand your limitations and then let's see if there are any solutions we can come up with to help get your application accepted,' I would have totally understood. That way, I would have been aware that I needed to get through more hoops than the average person, but that there was support and hope. Instead, I received a blanket response, 'No, you are disabled and could be a potential danger to yourself and others in our sport.' Once I reapplied, I got, 'OK, let's send someone round to his house to see how disabled this boy really is.' It was literally like that: 'How disabled are we talking?' Since my breakthrough, a more equal process has been created, which is great for anyone else trying to come through the pipeline. But for me as the first, let's just say things could have been handled better.

The stress of wondering whether or not the licence would come through before my first race weekend was just one more thing adding to the wild ride. By this point, word was starting to get out that I was going to be on the grid. When I signed to a team, it was big news within motorsport, because of my family and because of my condition. On top of that, the BBC found out about my participation and pitched a documentary which became a fly-on-the-wall programme about my first season. The excitement started to mount and I'm sure that kind of press attention factored into the MSA's decision on my licence. I had passed all the tests that they had asked of me, I had jumped through all the additional hoops on top of the unreasonable barriers to anyone trying to race. There would have been a lot of explaining to do if they hadn't let me race.

Of course, it goes without saying that my family's visibility helped swing the decision. I say use whatever tools you have at your disposal, but never take them for granted and never stop turning around to hold your hand back to help others through the door. Because of my experience, there are now several disabled drivers with licences. I know that seeing me do what I do every year has made it easier for people to follow in my path: it was like I was the thin end of the wedge. The following year, my licence was questioned again, and I had to go through another round of uncertainty before it was renewed, but since 2012 it has been reissued with no additional questions asked. To the point where I am now treated like any other driver in that process.

Finally, I received the go-ahead and was given the freedom to race. I went into my first weekend so high. The journey to that point had been like a game of snakes and ladders and at any time over those two months, it would have been easy to throw in the towel. So, to get on the grid for that first race was unreal. No, actually, it was *surreal.* You've got to remember that just two months before, I had been driving on a racing *game,* not able to use my legs effectively because they were not strong enough even for a game, and now there I was, actually racing in real life and *using* my legs. I didn't have the time or funds to do test days or anything like that, so I basically practised at the races themselves.

I qualified seventeenth and last for that first race, which was exactly what I had expected. I may have natural racing ability, but this was the real world. However, I was only two tenths of a second behind the next car ahead, which was much closer than I had thought I would be. That was amazing, because I knew I could improve by that amount at least, so there was a chance for me to beat other drivers in the future. That was all I had ever asked for, the chance to improve and see where I could go with it. By my second race weekend, I qualified fifteenth with three cars behind me and by the end of the year I'd made it up to mid-pack, qualifying eleventh, and was awarded 'driver of the weekend' as I achieved ninth and tenth places in my final two races. My rate of improvement was just incredible and shocked a lot of people, including my family, as they knew first-hand how inexperienced I was.

Going from being a teenager in his bedroom playing computer games to a recognized fixture in a sport that I had spent my entire life idolizing, in the space of two months, was impossible to process as it was happening. The number of people that I began to reach and who could see what I was doing was astounding. Obviously being related to Lewis turbocharged that, but the story didn't stop at who my brother was: they were interested in me because of the magnitude of what I was achieving. I had become a trailblazer in my own right and my rebellion against what was expected and accepted touched many other people's lives. After my first season, the documentary came out on the BBC in a prime-time slot, reaching 2.1 million views on that night, the most watched documentary that evening. It was then picked up by the airlines globally and was subsequently viewed 60 million times. I remember landing in the US after a long-haul flight and a fellow passenger seeing me in baggage reclaim. He said, 'It's Nicolas, right? I just saw your documentary on the flight. Wow, what a warrior you are – keep up the good work.'

When we talk about impact, that is a ridiculous feat for anyone, especially a disabled lad who should have been revising for his A-levels or planning to go to university. I struggled for a purpose when I was a kid. I didn't want to be disabled; I didn't want to be who I was. I just desperately wanted to be like everyone else. I didn't understand why it had to be me, why I was the one chosen to live with this condition. But by the time I turned 20, I had started to see a road ahead where I could use the person I was to help other people. That was no linear path, as you will discover through the lessons ahead, and I was still a long, long way from true acceptance and understanding of myself and the world around me. But the training wheels were off, I'd found that rebel within me – and I would never forget how it felt to race that car for the first time.

As you can probably appreciate, the whole 'Nic get a job!' situation had taken a bit of a back seat, as I was very fortunate to start my motorsport career. However, Dad was not going to let me get away with it that easily and still hounded me to do something in my spare time when I wasn't on the track – there is a lot of downtime in motorsport. So nearly two years later, I sat back down at the same kitchen table, but this time I wasn't drawing a blank. My mentality was totally different. I was a fully fledged racing driver, for crying out loud, who had already achieved so much by just driving a race car in the first place. I was a history maker. So, I used that confidence to see what I could come up with.

As I mentioned before, gaming was a huge part of my youth and I still spend a lot of time doing it, even today. So, I started to think about some game concepts and hatched an idea that would follow the transition from go-karts to Formula 1, based on the motorsport ladder. It turned out that there was already a game along similar lines in development by a company called Slightly Mad Studios, and after hassling them for a few weeks and trying to persuade them of my specific insight into that journey, I landed a job working as a Handling Consultant for the game Project CARS. The amazing thing was that the CEO of Slightly Mad Studios was one of the original founders of SimBin Studios, which developed GTR, RACE 07 and all the games that I used to play when I was younger. So, I went from being a customer and an avid fan to joining the development team on a new game and studio. It was like some kind of destiny.

My role as Handling Consultant was to take every car in the game, drive it and analyse it for realism. The whole point with any simulation game is for it to feel as close to reality as possible and since I had so much experience in the simulation racing world and now this added skill of driving in real life, I was the perfect person for the job. My day consisted of doing 50–100 laps in cars that the developers wanted me to test that week. I would analyse the car balance and behaviour, the authenticity of the tyre model, how the tyres felt during the different temperature processes, how they reacted and how it affected the car and balance. I would drive on the game for around eight hours a day and then write a detailed report of thousands of words on my findings. The developers would then make the changes based on my report, send the cars back to me and the process would start again. Dad had wanted me out of the house and off my computer; instead, I had achieved every teenage boy's dream job: I was getting paid to play video games in my bedroom. Bloody amazing!

PUSHING BACK AGAINST EXCLUSION: EVERYDAY ABLEISM

I get that the examples above are pretty elaborate and flashy. So let's dial it back to some more everyday circumstances and return to this idea of exclusion, something which I encounter often due to my disability. Take Friday night at the pub, for example. For most people, organizing a few drinks at the local boozer generally requires a few WhatsApps to your mates and agreeing a time to rock up. But for me, the story is a *liiiiittle* more complex, simply because my legs don't work the way the majority of other people's do. The biggest problems for me in any space are getting in, getting out, where the toilet is and what the seating situation is like. Handrails are always a gift; steps are always an obstacle. As someone who has lived in a wheelchair, I am also incredibly aware of when spaces do not cater for wheelchair users.

However, I never, ever, ever let anyone else's ignorance (or more often their lack of ambition to include me) exclude me or stop me from living a fulfilling life. When my friends have asked me to the pub, or a nightclub, I've never once said, 'Oh, I can't go, because they might not have a ramp or there are lots of steps.' Or, 'Can we meet somewhere else, there aren't any handrails in those bathrooms?' So, a place has made it difficult for me to enjoy time there? I always just think screw that and screw them – I'm going to make it work. I'm a true believer that you should never be embarrassed about who you are and what you have. I physically cannot change it, so I don't give two shits about what anyone thinks about me, or whether or not I'm particularly welcome somewhere. I'm still coming to the pub. That might mean that I end up 'problem solving' by sitting on my bum to get up high stairs, which understandably is something that a lot of people might feel uncomfortable about. If I were still in a wheelchair, it might mean asking my friends to help carry my weight. I totally get the embarrassment, but really the only embarrassment is that a space is inaccessible and excludes people like me. That is the shameful thing, not leaning on your bestie to get over the threshold. I'm not humiliated by a humiliating situation because I'm not going to let senseless barriers decide what I do or do not do. My presence in their space is the biggest rebellion I can make.

I have definitely seen a change in attitude and a new focus on accessibility in spaces like restaurants, but every week there will be a moment when I look around and I realize that if I hadn't got out of my wheelchair, I'd be done for, because the toilets are downstairs or there are no disabled toilets at all. The other day I went to a lovely restaurant with my family, but there were three steep steps to get on to the dining platform. For so many people, those three steps make all the difference. What they tell us is that our presence here hasn't been valued or considered. Yes, they made the restaurant look great, but in my eyes it had simply failed so many people.

While hospitality is beginning to open its eyes, what really gets to me is events. A major part of my career now is doing public-speaking events, something which brings me a huge amount of joy and has brought so much purpose to my life. But my God, events are incredibly inaccessible. You know when you go to a big do and there's a cocktail reception where everyone walks into a room and they just stand by these high tables? You're invited to enjoy two and a half hours of champagne or warm wine or whatever it is, and there's not a single chair or sofa in sight. Last year, I was speaking at an awards ceremony in front of 1,500 guests. Like nearly all of them, the event began with a cocktail reception which went on for hours as the ceremony was delayed. During that time, 1,500 people had not a single place to rest their weight. No one had thought that, out of 1,500 guests, there might be at least one who might need to sit at some point. Even among able-bodied people, there might be someone with a joint issue, dodgy knees or hips. Or someone recovering from an injury or illness. Someone on crutches or dealing with stamina issues.

Obviously, as a disabled person, you don't just want to be given a single seat on your own. If everyone else is standing up and you're at waist height it is invariably awkward, as they have to crouch to speak with you – something I know only too well from my time in a wheelchair. The point is there should be some sort of thought given – a sofa, a couple of chairs, something which can make you feel welcome and not excluded. I spend my life looking for a surface to lean on to take the stress and pain off my legs. And there is so often nothing. In the instance above, I was on my feet for three hours and the only way I could manage that was because I have trained myself to go through the pain. But what if people can't?

I mentioned this story in another speech a week or so later, as an example of where other people being oblivious to something so simple can make my life so difficult. After the speech, I was ushered to a room for cocktails, and guess what? Not a chair in sight. So many people came up to apologize, saying they had no idea and that it hadn't crossed their mind until I brought it up in my speech. They brought me a chair, which I made the decision not to sit on, as that would have singled me out. I don't say this to make anyone feel ashamed, I absolutely know it wasn't done out of malice, but I want to speak about my experiences so that people think just a little longer about those who have physical struggles.

Another space that is very keen to keep me out is retail. If you go along any busy street or to a mall, out shopping with your mates or your girl, as a disabled person who struggles physically on their feet, things get difficult almost immediately. There are a huge number of people, all trying to push past you, uneven pavements, holes and cobbles everywhere, which all mean I have to work extra hard when walking. For seating, the only good option is if the shop has a shoe section. But most of these luxury stores have everything on tables with no seating. I'm there, waiting for someone to try something on they probably won't even buy, and I end up leaning on displays next to a mannequin to rest my legs. Sometimes I sit on a step, or in the worst case I've sat on the floor. That's obviously not ideal, but again, the humiliation isn't on me – I've got to do what's right for me in that moment and it's not my fault I'm in this position. That's just how life is. Sometimes you are moved on by staff who don't want you leaning on a display. Often, I will have to go and find a coffee shop to sit down for a while before I can get it together, which is another energy-sapping process in itself, as sometimes the nearest spot is a trek away.

I often think that if the bosses of all these stores and fashion brands could live one day with my legs, things would change overnight. I know it would be easier for me just to stay home and accept that this kind of activity is too much for me. But even though these spaces don't cater for me, I'm not going to allow myself to be excluded, because I want to live a full life. Even so, I don't like it. Because it is *so* frequent, and such small changes could open up spaces and experiences to so many people.

There are many people like me living in-between an able-bodied and a disabled world. As someone who has been a wheelchair user in the past and now has the privilege of using my legs, I have an unusual understanding of both. Lots of people straddle the two and many of them were born able-bodied: those living with arthritis or struggling through pregnancy and post-natally, or cancer sufferers or someone who has been in an accident. Disability doesn't have to be a permanent state, but if we judge our society by its treatment of the most vulnerable, we can absolutely do better. While I will continue to rest my legs on tables stacked with tens of thousands of pounds' worth of designer goods, and if push came to shove would absolutely use whichever part of my body I needed to get up inaccessible stairs in high-end restaurants, my hope is that these acts of defiance will wake people up.

Is it everyone else's fault? No, not if their eyes haven't been opened to potential issues or struggles that disabled people face. You don't think about it if you don't *need* to think about it. But I want to make people aware. I'm not expecting everywhere I go to have some plush sofa waiting for me – it's not like I'm a diva. It's more knowing that there has been a consideration for anyone and everyone struggling. I've been excluded since day one and I've not been 'normal' from day one. The world has let it be known that I am not worthy of 'normal' access and treatment and, as a person brought into this world on the back foot, I could have internalized that I should expect nothing else. But I push back against this dynamic every day. There is next to nothing I don't feel I can do. Of course, I have my true limits. For example, my brother went on a trip to the Amazon a while back and that is just not something that would be open to me. The point is that all of us live with some kind of limitation, and the story of our lives is coming to terms with them.

There may be places where you too feel unwelcome, or spaces which don't seem to be open to someone like you, who looks like you, who went to a school like yours or grew up in the kind of house you did. People may very well judge you – but the only judgement that matters is the standard you set for yourself. Day to day, I have to push back against barriers and what other people think is appropriate or possible for me. But in doing so I have been able to carve out my own path.

Perhaps take a moment to think about the places and spaces which make you feel unwelcome and about some of the reasons behind that. Perhaps you dream of going to drama school, but when you go to the open day you don't see anyone who looks like you. Maybe they all have a different skin colour to yours. Perhaps you'd like to be a lawyer, but you watch the prospectus video and it seems like everyone speaks with a different accent and has come from a different background to yours. These thoughts are entirely natural, and I have had them all too. But just say to yourself: *Just because no one has done something before, it doesn't mean you can't be the first. Just because other people think you can't do something, doesn't mean you have to listen.*

Remember that Nic, the boy with CP in a wheelchair, is now a racing-car driver. He goes to the pub and to nightclubs and restaurants, even though there aren't any ramps. He speaks in front of thousands of people every week, inspiring them to shove their horizons higher. I absolutely believe that you can rebel like me and work towards your own goals. While you are doing that, keep front and centre the truth that other people's assumptions and judgements are just stories the world has taught them to believe *and* that you have the power to rewrite the narrative. Assumptions are bloody awful, and I know they're a really difficult thing to contend with in such a broad way. It's not just something that someone like me with disabilities has to deal with. It could be as small as living with a birthmark or a stammer or speech impediment. There are people who won't date other people based on a surname.

Speaking of assumptions, at school I wanted to be part of the basketball team. Initially there was some resistance – we can't have a disabled kid on our team, how would it possibly work? But again, employing the same tactics as I would later use on the MSA, I worked on the decision-makers, kept going back and didn't take no for an answer. Give me a shot. *Try me.* Let me show you. 'Oh, so he can actually get the ball in the net,' said those people who were ready with their nos. 'OK, he can't really dribble or run, but he has some kind of value.' Don't just assume that I won't be able to do something or that I will be a total liability to everybody else. Give me the shot to succeed or fail on my own terms. You just don't know. Sometimes (mostly) I don't know either, but you never know until you try. In the end, if you create your own story, the one that other people have been taught begins to fall away.

This is a lesson we also all need to take on board ourselves. When you see somebody, look for the potential rather than their apparent flaws. Give them a shot, whether that's in a job, a team or a new relationship. Once upon a time, I was more judgemental too – this is the world we have all been raised in and I was young and didn't have the same independence of mind. I definitely thought certain things of certain people when I didn't look at the bigger picture. When I was 17 or 18, I remember almost feeling like I was better than the average disabled person. I was stronger than them, I wasn't going to be pulled down or put into a box of disabled people and I strived to be as normal as I could be with my condition, because I felt that the more able-bodied I could see myself mentally, the more other people's perception of me would be accepting.

But now I see how incredibly judgemental that was. As we are all living with such different experiences, there really is no comparison to be made.

Comparisons based on assumption begin so early, often in school with really young kids who are made to feel that there are already doors closed to them before they have even begun. Kids are judged at such a ridiculously young age – I felt like I was written off as a five-year-old. It happened to Lewis, too – no one believed that he would get anywhere, and now look at him. Look at us both. As a society, people will judge children's potential before they can even read and write. As well as pushing back rebelliously against this framework, I really want you to try to change your own mindset in terms of how you judge everyone else. Everyone is meant to get a go. Everyone deserves a chance. When you have the power to challenge an assumption about anyone else, take it and give them a shot. Of course, it might fail, but equally it might not, and you will help them rewrite the expectations.

Of the many things that I'm proud about in terms of the man I have become, perhaps the most important is how empathetic and understanding I have learned to be and how often I give people chances to prove the world wrong – even if sometimes that leads to getting a whole load of grief in return. There's no point demanding a chance yourself if you can't give it to someone else too – what needs to change is the whole systemic make-up of access to opportunity.

HOW YOU CAN BE A REBEL TOO

Finding the confidence to say the rules don't matter and I'm going to make my own rules isn't some overnight epiphany. Firstly, you have to understand that when you are knocked back, the feelings of rejection and neglect you're going through are totally normal and valid. Secondly, it's not your fault if you have been turned down because of what someone else believes in, rather than the truth of who you are and what you can do in this moment. Perhaps they don't have the imagination or experience to think outside of the stories they have been brought up to believe. That is their current limitation. But, if it's not your fault, it's time to shake yourself off and start the steps towards getting in control of where you want to go *regardless of what people say or think*.

If you've been rejected and you still want to do something, you have to give it a go at least once more. I would like to say you have to *keep* trying until you get there, but I understand that the emotional toll of this can be deep. So, let's start with at least once more. There is no point talking about it and saying I would love to do x, y or z and not doing it because someone told you 'no' once. I don't care if it's your friends or family who told you that – it's your life, it's your decision.

Next up, begin to break down what it will take for you to get closer to your ambition without anyone else's say so and start at step one. I look at life like a ladder, which means you've got to start on the first rung in order to get anywhere. When I set myself a goal, the first thing I do is zoom out and think about every little micro movement between where I am now and the top of that ladder. Let's take my racing to start off with. OK, so I want to race in British Touring Cars, how do I do that? I know I need a race licence, but that's not the first step, because to even get in the car I need some money. To get money I need to start approaching people who spend on sponsorship. How do I find out about that? And then how do I make those contacts? Before I even start trying to speak to potential contacts, I need a presentation. To build a presentation, I need skills. To gain skills, I need a computer. To get a computer, I need to earn some money. You might be fortunate to have savings to buy this computer, or maybe you need to go out and find a job. That is the first step. This is you learning to invest in yourself and your ambitions. On day zero, you have to work on the first step, because there is no way to the top of the ladder without your initial move. There is no rocket pack that will fly you up there. You've got to buy that computer; you've got to create that presentation. Focusing on step one allows you to block out the negative voices and make a start. Make that plan, quietly if you would prefer, and take on everything in small, manageable stages.

It has taken me seven years to have a consistent career. I have failed so many times. I've been knocked back and down and I have seen what rock bottom looks like. There have been times when I believed that the voices of both people who love me and people who hate me were right and I was wrong. But then this little spark kept relighting and this rebellious spirit started to burn again until a voice whispered, you know what? You know you can do this. Just take the next step. If you don't have that voice yourself, I hope you can hear mine whispering to you too. It's never too late.

One of the hardest things, if you spend enough time around people who aren't open to new stories and ways of doing things, is that they can start draining your energy and your spirit. They can make you feel different about yourself. They can take pieces of you away. You can so easily get deterred or change your direction because of what someone who doesn't know you as well as you know yourself thinks of you and your potential. We all need to do what *we* feel, not what other people *think*. I could think to myself, should I really go out there and do this, because they're probably going to think this or that of me? Should I really go out there on the grid or on the stage in front of hundreds of people? What if I fall? But at the end of the day, who cares what they think? Yours is the only face you have to stare back at in the mirror. To be able to turn around and say, actually, no, I am not the sum of what you think or who you are perceiving me to be, takes a lot of strength.

One way to tap into this inner resolve is to surround yourself with the people who give you the support and the strength to continue growing. Walking away from or at least muting the people who are sucking your energy and spirit is another one of the hurdles you have ahead. But it's an active choice you have to make. You can't just sit around and wait for someone to give you permission to take the first step up that ladder, and you can't prove the haters wrong by wishing it was so.

At the end of every year I didn't get there, I would sit down and evaluate what had blocked my path and how I could have applied myself differently and better. *I can make it happen, next year I'll be closer.* If last year I did x wrong, next year I'm going to change it. So much of my success has been this kind of trial and error and taking failure like a punch to the gut before standing back up and heading back in for more. I don't have the silver bullet to make this process quicker. Every one of our dreams is different, as are our personalities and talents, so your journey is going to look very different from mine. But if you go into those seemingly hard-to-reach dreams knowing that there's a good chance things are going to be hard, that at times you're going to be demoralized and have to pick yourself back up, you will have a more realistic idea of what it's going to feel like. Failure is how I characterize the early years of success. Perhaps even total and utter abject failure. Get used to failure, make it your friend, and definitely don't fear it. Everything is a failure until you succeed, so just keep going.

Then one day, perhaps completely out of the blue, you will feel the momentum begin to shift. A door will open. And while it's not going to be like a slide from there into your dreams, it will begin to change how you feel about yourself. The moment that you're like, shit, this is happening, I'm getting somewhere, is so exhilarating, but you have to keep climbing the rungs of the ladder until you actually get to where you are heading. I've still got mountains to climb myself, but when I look up, the top of the mountain is much closer than it once was.

People have told me no many, many times along this road. It's almost like it's the only word I seem to get. Do you think I could? . . . No. Would you mind? . . . No. Could it be possible to? . . . No. Everything is a no. You have to take their no and turn it into your yes. If it feels as though you are literally the only person who thinks you can achieve a certain goal and every other human being on the planet says you can't, guess what? You still can.

There is always a chance.

Equally, I need to be crystal clear about this: failures and setbacks can be incredibly hard to deal with mentally. In 2022, I fell back into a dark place after losing my main racing sponsor, then very quickly seeing their name on the side of someone else's car. It is like your girlfriend breaking up with you and you seeing her with her new boyfriend almost immediately. It made me feel so incredibly rubbish. The old feelings of worthlessness crept back in: why do I have to have all these things wrong with me, why do I have this condition, why am I denied all the time? I let the whispers, the negative ones, take over. During this period, I was on a family holiday at a ski resort. I ski in a chair – an adaptive mono-ski, if you will. I am pretty badass at it, to be fair, and have been skiing for years. However, this particular time, the chair had a part missing. Lewis had been building it for hours and was so excited for me to come out on the slopes with him. But for some reason, while watching it all unfold, I just couldn't bear it. It was taking so much stress and time to build the damn thing, just so I could do something that everyone else does without even thinking. I lost it and uncharacteristically burst into tears in front of my family.

It was my dad who first consoled me and said that he thought every day about the way I was brought into the world and wishes he could do something to change it for me. He wished that he could take it away for me, but no matter how much he wishes he could, he will never be able to. Thinking about the emotional weight that my parents have been carrying around, but never once let on about when I was growing up, or made me feel a burden, helped rally me. For a few minutes, I let it all pile on top of me, but it passed. It is totally normal to have those moments and we all let the negativity in from time to time. None of us is a machine and just because things go well for a while it doesn't mean your demons just vanish.

As well as offering tons of support, my family have tried to steer me in different directions and to put me off making a huge range of decisions. But from the day I started to develop my own understanding of how life works, I have always come to those conclusions alone. Yes, your parents only want the best for you. *But* what they think is the best for you might not always be the case or take into account the ladder you're on. The only way you can be true to yourself is to connect to that instinct, the feeling in your gut. That lurching, heaving feeling of almost sickness when you think about giving up on something you are passionate about. That is something you always have to listen to, no matter what advice you are receiving, even when it comes with a full heart behind it. If I had taken my parents' advice as gospel, I wouldn't have made it to where I am now either. Through their love they basically taught me how to use my middle finger and, with my deepest respect and love, I've had to metaphorically show it back to them from time to time. They inspired me to find the courage to be able to stand up and voice that I can hear what they're saying, but I'm going to go in my own direction and do what I want to do regardless of how it goes, bad or good. That takes guts for anyone.

While I don't wake up every morning and think, 'Oh no, I'm disabled', I do wake up every day with a disability. And with that there's either a new problem that's come up or an older problem that has re-emerged. Sometimes I can be dealing with 10 different pains from different areas of my body at once. At the time of writing, I'm dealing with an issue with a bone in my foot, which is the main source of my current pains. It's always bloody something. Even though I have progressed so far, when issues arise I don't feel less disabled than I did when I was a child. While I'm physically stronger now, the underlying issues have never changed. The things that I struggle with now are what I struggled with as a kid. General movement, balance, walking up and down steps. But my mentality has so completely changed that it has fundamentally shifted my relationship with my disability, the thing that I had always believed was holding me back from living a full life. When I was a kid, I didn't know the alternative ways to do things and get from A to B, and I didn't want to look different or disabled or like I was struggling. I wanted to be cool and fit in. I wanted girls to like me, and I couldn't imagine any girl falling for a guy who sometimes had to sit on his bum to get up the stairs. A lot *has* changed, such as my legs being stronger today and being able to walk longer distances. I fall over less and I'm *completely* independent. But in a nutshell, the condition is exactly the same – I just know how to deal with it and with a different mindset I have turned my lemons into lemonade by building a career around what is unique about me.

The first time I was asked to speak about my journey, I didn't even know that public speaking was an industry. I just turned up, said what I had to say and, even though I'd never done anything like it before, I thought it went OK. In the crowd, unbeknown to me, there was someone who worked for a speaking bureau, which is like an agency for speakers. That day they got in touch, signed me straight away and since then this entirely new career has just snowballed. Even though I had no aspirations to do it – mostly because I simply didn't know it existed – it has become one of the most fulfilling aspects of my life. I never knew that my life's challenges would ever translate to something which means so much to so many people. When I think of the shame that I once carried about all my experiences, it is truly shocking to me that I now speak publicly to thousands of people about those things. Once upon a time, all I wanted to do was hide those moments and move on from them. But as I have rebelled – against what I was brought up by society to feel, that being disabled is embarrassing, or that walking the way I walk is humiliating, or I should try to blend in and never stand up or out about who and what I am – I have found more and more strength and power in my voice.

USE YOUR VULNERABILITIES AS A WEAPON OF REBELLION

I can remember from a fairly young age understanding that vulnerability had its own power. When I was around eight years old, I was really struggling to come to terms with my condition, who I was and why. I used to cry myself to sleep every night because I was so different from everyone else around me. I just didn't understand why it had to be me who was the oddball. My mum would always try to pick me up and would never let me get down. She would say, 'Nic, you need to realize that you are a unique person and as time goes on, and you get stronger, you will understand your limitations but also how to capitalize on your individuality.' She would also say that all able-bodied people walk the same, but I had something special. It's just me and that makes it precious.

So many of us were raised to believe that our limitations and insecurities weaken us, so we have to try to hide them from the world, even from ourselves. Turning that around to reframe and rebrand the things that I was once scared, unsure or ashamed of is certainly a work in progress for me, but celebrating *difference* rather than weakness is an act of rebellion. Reminders of my limitations, both big and small, are always lurking at every corner. The minute I step out of my home, there will be a child staring or an obstacle in my path, or I'll feel pain from one thing or another, so I simply can't escape my vulnerabilities – they are there every day for everyone to see. It might be at bigger moments that you feel your limitations have really let you down, like when you're sitting an important exam or presenting in public. But it is also in the everyday – perhaps not being able to get on an overfull bus or, for me, knowing that I just have to sit down somewhere on a trip out with a friend. There are denials and negative moments in nearly every day. What's important is being able to put your feelings of frustration to one side and calmly accept that things aren't always going to go your way. Everyone has limitations of some sort, and no one is accepted everywhere by everyone 24/7. If you start to focus too much on the things you can't do, or struggle to do, if you start to obsess about all the ways in which your skills or personality or abilities limit you, *that* is when your disadvantages can overwhelm you.

Instead, I always do my very best not to get frustrated, but to reappraise my unique set-up. I know that my struggles with movement have made me a more empathetic person, have led me to build this extraordinary career, have enabled me to connect with and inspire so many people. That is a superpower, so how can I truly see it as a weakness?

And as you already know, I don't believe that denial should ever feel set in stone. Rejection and failure *are* parts of life, but that doesn't mean they're the end of the road. Expect rejection, but never hesitate to challenge with a healthy dose of rebellion when you feel that the rejection is unwarranted, that it's just because someone has said that your 'limitations' mean you can't do something. Turn the story around and show how your differences actually make you uniquely placed to bring a different perspective or attitude to a situation. If you are nervous when speaking in public, tell your audience and they will empathize with you. That simple act of sharing your vulnerability might change someone else's perspective and make them feel more confident next time they have to stand up in front of people, and

I guarantee they will listen to you more and with more kindness – there is such power in that. If you know that exams make your brain turn to mush, explore other ways of assessment, and look into any other opportunities to prove your worth. Perhaps you can use your challenges to begin your cover letter to get work experience in your chosen industry – there are enough other people out there who have struggled with exams to mean you will probably find a kindred spirit who can help you.

Obviously that isn't going to work in every single situation, but don't let your limitations be the main story that you tell to yourself or to anyone else. Keep asking the questions, keep pushing your foot into doors. It only takes one person to walk through and change the story. We can all be rebels, just by taking one step at a time.

Takeaways

* In both big and small ways, you are going to encounter obstacles to achieving what you want in your life. This is a given, it's not personal, so try to stop taking it that way. What I want you to know is that even if these barriers seem set in stone, you always have the right to rebel against them.
* You are the company you keep, or at least you are to a certain extent. When you want to do something which the world believes isn't possible for you, an important factor can be the people around you and how they respond to your ambitions. While I preach a lot about the value of your internal voice, listening all day long to people who don't support your dreams and try to pull you back down can be incredibly draining. Listen to how others respond

to your aspirations and choose carefully who you share them with. A final caveat – even if no one else believes in you, you can still believe in yourself.

* A vulnerability is not the same as weakness. We can all feel as if things in our make-up or nature are a liability, but I challenge you instead to see those areas as a special reserve of tenderness. Drill down to what your so-called failings are really all about and work immediately on reframing them. Perhaps you feel you struggle with organization? But doesn't that make you more spontaneous and able to adapt and be flexible? I'm not saying don't work on skills which you find hard, more stop beating yourself up about them and turn the difficulty on its head.

LESSON TWO

ALWAYS WALK THE HARDEST PATH

We live in a convenience era. Fancy a sandwich for lunch? Just use an app. Need to get a gift for your mum? It's one click away. I do it, you do it. It's the way life is today. The problem with this is that it's *very* easy to get used to things being 'easy'. And that, as I know from experience, can be a very slippery slope. What I have learned the painful way is that *nothing* worth having in life comes without a bit of friction. However tempting – and it can be incredibly tempting – it may be to follow the path of least resistance, it is nearly always a trap. I have always seen the value of things being hard, because from a very young age I have seen the results you can achieve by taking the harder route. That doesn't mean I always followed through with what I'd learned, though, and it took me many years of avoiding hard things to cement this habit into my mentality. But now it is there, it has become the bedrock on which my self-esteem, my identity and, I believe, my many successes have been built.

YOU ARE ALWAYS MORE THAN A DIAGNOSIS

As I mentioned earlier, when I was still tiny, my doctors told my parents that I would most likely spend the rest of my life in a wheelchair or, 'at best', walk with a stick. For many years, I found myself on the road that had been prescribed for me. Before I share any more of this part of my story, I want to stress that I have huge, unending understanding and empathy with people who are dealing with all manner of physical and mental challenges. It's all well and good me talking about hard and easy, but none of us is working with the exact same issues and each and every one of our bodies presents a whole new context.

Instead, what I am talking about in this lesson is the importance of continuing to be ambitious for yourself and striving every day to reach for your *true* upper limits, no matter what they are or what your abilities. It's about not discounting a route or a goal because it is hard, it's about seeing the hardest path as most likely the right one and one that is available to you even if people try to steer you in another direction. There is this magical space somewhere between ambition and fantasy which should be encouraged and supported, and that goes for every child, every person, no matter what their background, not just those who struggle with their abilities. I also want to acknowledge that not everyone is driven by bigger ambitions and if you are entirely happy and content in where you are in life, all power to you. But if you *do* want more for yourself and you *do* wish you could achieve all kinds of goals, I want to share my experience and the philosophy that has driven me to overcome awesome and seemingly insurmountable challenges.

My parents received the news that I had CP when I was 18 months old, after they realized I had missed some key developmental milestones. Every movement I made with my legs, I made by using them both at the same time, instead of alternately. Crawling, I would drag both legs, in a baby walker I would use both legs, but I could only push myself backwards and not forwards. When standing, I would be on my tiptoes and not able to put my heels down. Initially, after the diagnosis, my mum went through a hard stage of blaming herself for my premature birth. Of course, it was no one's fault, but as a parent it is so natural to beat yourself up for not being able to protect your kid. However, pretty quickly, both Mum and Dad reached a point where they decided that they had to accept our position and look to my future. From my earliest years, my parents had a vision for what my life would look like when I was in my thirties, the age I am today. They weren't thinking solely about how I was going to be as a toddler or even a teenager – it was how I was going to be able to live as an adult that mattered, and that meant focusing on my ability to be independent from them from the get-go. The translation of this was that I was about to start at the school of hard knocks.

Controversially in some circles, one part of their philosophy meant that they didn't pick me up when I fell, and a kid with CP falls over a *lot*. When I fell down, they would never ever panic or run to catch me. Dad always said, 'Keep going, keep going, you will get there,' and even when I asked for help, he would say, 'No, I'm not always going to be here, you have to learn to do this for yourself.' I remember Mum would tell me, 'Nic, you're fine, brush yourself off.' I was the opposite of mollycoddled, because my parents believed that overprotecting me would limit what I would be able to achieve one day. Just because I was disabled didn't mean they were always going to hold my hand. In their minds, it was unfortunate that my situation was more challenging than most, but that didn't mean they would blithely make allowances for me, or – they believed – I would never gain the strength I would need one day. They were tough on me in ways which probably go against most people's instincts and certainly go against the grain of modern parenting culture, especially when it comes to a child with a disability.

But from day one, Mum and Dad took a decision which they hoped would stretch me and, for better or worse, that is exactly what it did. After the initial prognosis was delivered, they made up their minds that they weren't going to accept absolutely everything my doctors had told them. I want to be entirely respectful and say how indebted I am to the medical profession, for the surgery I had as a child and the care I have received over the years from all kinds of doctors and specialists. I have no animosity or resentment towards doctors, far from it. What I do believe, however, is that we all share a bit of a misconception about diagnostics and prognosis. When a child with CP walks into a doctor's office, as I did, to the doctor that kid will be another data point on a curve of boys and girls with mobility issues. They will draw from their experience and the case studies they have read and will tell parents that their child's condition will affect them in this way and that, and that they will struggle with x and y. They will zero in on average expectations and paint a picture of limitations based on precedent. Scared and inexperienced parents will take this information as law and will frame their children's potential through this matrix of limitations.

What I want to remind everyone is that there is always hope for each individual to have an outcome that isn't predicated by the book. While professionals obviously do not want to raise false hopes around health issues, no one can feel out your limits except you. No doctor can predict the role of determination or personality when they are trying to convey expectations from what they've learned in data sets. Statistics are never going to be able to encompass the individual. There is not a doctor on this planet who, when I was an infant, would have told my parents not to worry because one day I would be driving racing cars. There are probably very few who would have told them I would be able to walk unaided or live a totally independent life. But here I am, defying all those expectations every single day.

The way I like to think of it is as a bit like racing. In racing, you have the driver and you have the engineer, who work together as a team. The engineer has done thousands and thousands of hours of training and endless courses and gained a huge education in how to set up a race car. If things aren't going in the right direction, they will know what should be changed, based on what the manual says. Conversely, the driver can *feel* what's not right. Or what they want. It's their decision how they want to drive the car or how they want the car to behave. Perhaps they want to go by the book and listen only to what the engineer has to say, but perhaps they can feel something else. Doctors know so much and have invested a huge amount of time and energy into their learning. But they can only know the book. They can't *feel* what you can.

For parents of kids with ability challenges, I really want to say, keep being ambitious for your children. Bring them up in a framework where nothing is off limits until they've tried it. Believe in the power of their spirit to turn the book on its head. For everyone else, this is a lesson which can apply to us all. Do not let average expectations of 'people like you' box you in. Be conscious and aware of how these messages might have influenced you through your life, making you believe you are incapable of certain things, and know that you have the chance to fight back against them and write your own script. It might mean you taking the hardest road.

My parents made the decision that they would treat me as a normal boy as much as they possibly could and that meant there were some hard moments for me. I started my education at a regular nursery, but by that point I was in a walking frame. I can remember loving that frame – my mum let me do pretty much whatever I wanted when I was using it, and she never put a lid on my adventures or desire to explore. I used to walk with my frame, but every time there was a downhill slope, I'd run and then sit on the back of it, hurtling downwards. Initially people would panic when they saw me do it, but they soon learned that I was fine and having the best time. My mum taught me that even if I fell, it was OK. If I thought of having a cry and my bottom lip was quivering, she would reassure me that actually it was all right. I soon learned to sit on my frame, fall, land on my hands, brush myself down and get back up. Seeing my resilience not only changed people's perception, but crucially I began to build my confidence in my own abilities.

By the time I got to primary school, being around able-bodied kids was all I knew. I'd actually never met another disabled person in my life up to that point, which was sometimes a little lonely, but also not really something I thought about very much. My parents could have enrolled me at a special-needs school, but they chose not to. They chose to send me to a regular comprehensive primary school, because mentally I wasn't affected at all by my condition. As it was all physical, they felt I would be able to deal with it.

The school itself was very welcoming straight away. I always had a helper in my class if I had any difficulty keeping up – this would usually be around writing, which was more physically taxing for me than it is for most people. During every single lunch break, while all the other kids were playing, I would be doing stretches with the same helper, Mrs Wood, and working on my physio to loosen my muscles and build my strength. She was a fabulous person and helper for me – the only thing I couldn't get my head around was that she always had *freeeezing* cold hands every time we did my stretches! Even back then I was constantly battling to overcome my condition, but it was harder because I was too young to fully understand the reasoning behind it all.

Through my years at primary school, I had started to walk without my frame and mostly I was supported in that by my teachers and classmates. Yes, kids would stare and that would make me feel a bit odd and rubbish, but by that time I had sort of come to accept that as part of life. When you haven't seen something new before, you stare, but when you see it every day, it just becomes normal. You're used to it. And I made a best friend for life on my first day. His name was Ben.

Back then, Ben was this tall and lanky, super-popular lad and we just instantly clicked and got on like a house on fire. Because Ben was treated 'normally', when he befriended me and invited me into the group, everyone else accepted me too. I remember the first time he asked me over to his house and introduced me to his family: his mum Sarah, dad John, brother Tom, and sister Alice. They didn't have absolutely everything, but they were such good people, worked hard and welcomed everyone into their home, which is where I think Ben gets his kind nature from. In our two-decades-plus friendship, he has never made me feel that my disability is an issue and has always just accepted me for exactly who I am.

Ben was my support mechanism through my early years at school. At the time, I lived a long way from school, whereas he was right in the same neighbourhood. When I went home, that was it; I only ever saw my friends at school. But Ben got home and then went straight out again to play football on the green with his mates. I spent a lot of time at his house (and he came to mine a lot too) and he brought me into his circle after school as well. He would *always* include me. That was such a huge support for me as a young kid, because he provided a gateway for me: sharing his equality stopped me feeling like an outsider and protected me from any kids who wanted to exclude me. It taught me from a really young age that there were good people in the world and that I would be able to build friendships, even with the limits of my condition.

Both my parents and my school really supported me just getting stuck in with everything. So, I would do PE and football and basketball and rugby alongside all the able-bodied kids. It was never a question of doing a disabled version of whatever game to help Nic fit in. Ben played for a local football club and I decided I wanted to do it too. So, I started to play for the team, even though I literally couldn't kick a ball to save my life. I never got the ball in a game and obviously no one would pass it to me because I wouldn't be able to do anything with it. But I had my football boots on, I was part of the team and I was running around the pitch.

To me, I was playing football. The governing body allowed our team 12 players on the pitch instead of 11 and I would go to football training every Wednesday. Mum would stand on the side of the pitch, frozen to the core, and never, ever complained, even though she must have seen that I clearly had no talent for the beautiful game. She knew it was something that gave me confidence and a sense of acceptance, so she stuck to it with me and never made me feel like it wasn't normal for me to be doing it.

EVERYONE HAS A METAPHORICAL CHAIR

With a lot of work in physio, I was able to get by without a wheelchair right up to the age of 11. But at secondary school, that all changed because the demands suddenly became much more physical. Even though, thanks to all that physio, I was as loose and straight as I had ever been, the sheer size of my new school was far beyond what I was used to. Getting from A to B across such long distances between classes while also carrying a heavy bag was unrealistic, as at that age I just hadn't yet had the chance to build enough strength and stamina to cope with such a gruelling physical routine. Initially, I did try to make it work, but I was tearing through trainers weekly and arriving late to every class, completely physically drained and drenched with sweat through my uniform. I was destroyed by the end of the week. My legs were in acute pain, and I was finding it impossible to take anything in study-wise – it was just so much to manage and completely unsustainable.

So, reluctantly, we brought a wheelchair to school and I would store it in the staff room. I continued to always walk at home, but inevitably, as I walked less during the day, my legs became weaker and it became harder and harder to be mobile across long distances.

What's more, I got used to the convenience and started to really lean into that – I started taking the easy road. I stopped bothering to do anything to counter the impact my chair was having on my progress, I stopped pushing myself to do more physio or strength training to make up for the time I was spending on my bum. In fact, rather than trying to reduce the number of activities I did in my chair, so I could become strong enough not to use it, I relied on it more and more. When I went racing with Lewis, I started to bring my chair and I suppose, for want of a better word, I became a bit lazy with it. I was even using my chair to go out to dinner when we were away, which is ridiculous as you're sat down most of the time anyway. The problem with sitting back into any kind of 'chair' in life is that if you don't use it, you lose it, and the result for me was that by the time I was 16 I was constantly in my wheelchair. For my mum, because she knew I could walk and I did walk at home, I'm not sure it really registered how much my muscles had deteriorated, though she did often tell me how the chair was actually making my life more difficult. But in so many ways, it was *such* a relief to sit in that chair, because I didn't have to try so hard. I had been stretching myself both literally and metaphorically my whole life. There hadn't been a day which hadn't been a struggle and I was so tired of the fight.

I think everyone can relate to this story in some way. While you may never have struggled with your mobility, doubtless there have been times in your life when you have reached a crossroads and taken the opportunity to take the easier path. Who hasn't, at some point, sat back in their own metaphorical chair? Perhaps you decided to stop trying at a subject at school because you found it hard. Maybe you dropped all your language lessons, for example. Or maybe you'd wanted to play for the football team and worked really hard until a little injury laid you up for a week and for whatever reason you never got back into the routine. Perhaps you decided to pass on an opportunity for promotion because you felt the mountain was too high to climb, so you backed out. It's easy to give up on things. It's easy to excuse yourself for doing it, too, especially when you feel exhausted with the effort you've been putting in – I know, because I did it. The problem is that one of these days you might find yourself needing the things you gave up. That dream job that you missed out on because you couldn't speak French. The camaraderie and connection of the football team which you couldn't recreate. The chance to be challenged by a new role if only you could have been just that bit more determined. If you give up on things you want, you run the risk of regret. In so many ways, it is better to see things through, to push until you have no breath left in you, and then and only then, when every single avenue has been exhausted, can you say, I gave it my all, but it wasn't meant to be.

While I had initially given my mobility my all, I had now stopped giving it anything. Part of me decided to accept what I'd always been told my limits were. Knowing that doctors had said I would probably be in a wheelchair all my life had almost become a self-fulfilling prophecy. I had totally internalized the ceiling set by someone else. There isn't much of a line between easy and idle – and I absolutely don't mean that as disparagement, so many of us are brought up to believe that easy and friction-less are the best and, especially when we have a disability and everything is so damn hard every day, it is incredibly tempting to just go for that route. Somewhere inside, I knew I was letting myself down, but I pushed that kind of thought to the back of my mind and made excuses to myself every time for not being bothered to walk or do my physio.

It's like the pendulum had swung the entire other way – after years of battling, I waved the white flag.

But the truth is, while the chair did make some elements, especially the logistics, easier, my mum was right. Limiting my ability to walk made so many other areas of my life harder. As a 15- or 16-year-old, all I wanted to do was be like every other teenager. I wanted to go out and just be a lad, you know. My mates were all becoming lads and going out and having a few drinks and getting drunk. And I wasn't doing any of that because of my chair, because I felt as if there wasn't a place for me in it in any of those spaces. I was also nervous about getting alcohol – what would it do to my mobility and coordination? The first time I got drunk was on 'Blue WKD' when I was 18! I made sure that I was with someone I trusted and chose my cousin Nathan, who is like a brother to me. I had absolutely no idea what to expect, but all I knew was that he would be able to look after me if 'shit hit the fan'. As it turns out, I *can* walk when drunk, it's just quite a bit harder and even more wobbly! Of course, I'd also started to feel attracted to girls and really wanted a girlfriend, but I thought I was never going to get one, feeling the way I did about myself. My steps backwards in my mobility had really taken a toll on my self-esteem and put me back in the position of 'odd one out'. It felt like girls would only want to be with someone cool or popular, all those on-the-surface things which are so important at secondary school. In my head, I formed the narrative that I had no *choice* but to be in my chair, and because I believed that no girl would want to be with me in it, I became really bitter and resentful against the world. I definitely went through a phase of thinking all able-bodied people were arseholes, but really that was because my self-esteem was so low. I knew deep down that I needed to do something to change things, but because life was so much easier for me physically in my chair and the mountain to climb seemed so huge, I couldn't get out of the rut. To be fair, it *was* huge. It wasn't easy life vs. slightly tricky life. It was easy life vs. a literal nightmare. At that low point it felt impossible to even think about getting there.

MAKE DAY ONE TODAY

The turning point came for me on another trip racing with Lewis. It was, as I've found so often is the case with watershed moments, a very small incident that sparked the shift in gear, something which perhaps only I would have ever noticed. I was 16 years old and we were at the airport as a family checking in. Mum had pushed me to the desk and, as happened so often when I was in my chair, the woman behind the check-in desk acted as if I was invisible and addressed my mum to talk about me. 'Mrs Hamilton, does your son require assistance?' she asked, as if I were a tiny child. It wasn't the first time it had happened, by any means, but for some reason this time in particular stung and made me feel utterly humiliated. I was a 16-year-old young man and full of all the associated hormones. I knew I was my own person, with my own voice and thoughts. While I wasn't technically an adult, I could certainly speak for myself or answer a question. The immediate instinct in these situations can be to feel rage towards the person ignoring you, against the world for discriminating against you, against people who might lack empathy to consider how their treatment could make you feel. But the real rage burning was directed at myself, because in my heart of hearts I knew my decision to rely on my wheelchair was enabling her overlooking of me. I knew I had it in me to physically get myself up. I had been pushing my bodyweight for years, so I was strong from an upper body stand point, but my legs were far too weak *in that moment*. But that woman's treatment of me that day made me see that I had been metaphorically treading water. Through that one short interaction, I had come to a new realization, and I decided it was time to take responsibility for myself and my situation as much as I possibly could. That was it. This was not how I wanted to live my life any more.

After that trip, I never used my wheelchair again.

The hurt, the graft, the battle encompassed by the sentence above is something which is really hard to convey. The first part of rejecting my wheelchair was walking, putting one foot in front of the other. It seems so simple when it's something you do every day. I barely think about it these days. But when you have weak legs – and mine were like mush, with no substance to them – each part of the multiple movements that your body puts together to create a step is a process you have to master. Picking up your leg is just the first part; you've also got to clear the floor with your trailing leg and maintain an upright balance while you are moving through the transfer of weight. At the beginning, I was falling over all the goddamn time because I could only lift my legs to such a shallow height that I'd trip over any little thing. Falling over when you're little is socially seen as normal, but falling over as a teenager or adult is something different, so I had to get used to the attention that brought – as well as focusing on not falling over the entire time. You also have to learn how to fall really well when it goes wrong, which it does often. You have to bounce or roll with it and very quickly you have to learn to not land on your head or break your wrists. For me at least, I had to get used to cutting my hands and bleeding several times a day.

I suppose, along with my legs, I'd let my ability to work through pain soften, so I had to toughen up again to deal with the huge amount of discomfort which was to become my every day.

Absolutely nothing about my shift from my chair to walking was planned or mapped out. There wasn't any kind of transition programme or expert guidance. It was cold turkey, from zero to a hundred in one day. I didn't build myself up to it either physically or mentally, I didn't seek specialist opinion. I didn't even tell my mum what I was going to do. I just turned up to school that morning and didn't get my chair from the staff room. I knew it was going to suck, and it really did. It was *brutal*. During those early weeks I had never-ending cuts on my hands and knees, and I was just physically a mess. The muscle pain was relentless as the fibres were torn and torn again in the process of building, and there wasn't a moment for weeks and weeks when my muscles didn't ache. There were days when I'd wake up and just think, I can't do it again. Other times, the pain would wake me up in the night. But I knew from experience that the pain in my muscles was the right kind of pain, the type of pain that meant I was getting stronger again.

Pretty quickly my mum did start to notice (the injuries might have been a bit of a giveaway), but she could also see that my legs were looking straighter and that I was walking with more ease. My mum has this instinct when I'm walking with her, to look out for any obstacle and tell me to watch it. When I was learning, I was so focused on my balance that sometimes I couldn't combine that with looking where my feet were going and I'd trip on uneven ground or fall down a step. My poor mum would go from just casually walking to having 'cat-like' reflexes where I would end up hanging off her – I couldn't stop myself. Mum would be trying to hold me up and I'd be swinging on her arm, which was really bad for her, but we just laughed together, as I was swinging from her like a monkey from a branch while I tried to get my feet underneath me again. As she noticed my progress and my legs got stronger, the swinging episodes happened less and less, so she started to take away her support.

After building up my strength and confidence to get back on my feet at school, my thoughts turned to what I would physically need if I were to actually have a girlfriend – something I'd missed out on by withdrawing during the time I was in my chair. If I was going to be holding her hand, the last thing I wanted to be doing was pulling her over or swinging from her on our first date, or any date for that matter, so I had to learn not to tug when I was taking someone's support, almost like a dog on a lead. I did extra physio when I got to about 17 or 18, which really supported the process of getting back to where I had been, and stronger, and I used to wear splints at night, which put my legs straight out in front of me to stretch my hamstrings. But it really was the walking that built the strength back up. I was coming home battered and bruised, but I knew it was progress. The more I walked, the less I fell.

After getting to a level at school, the next phase was walking up and down the stairs at home and seeing whether I could do five steps without losing my balance. I used to have to touch the banister for support, but as time went on, I challenged myself to go up the stairs by taking one finger away at a time for less support, until I got to the stage where I could do it hardly holding on at all. Doing that exercise again and again and again made a massive difference overall with my balance and eventually I could do a whole staircase not holding on to anything. That was a *huge* achievement.

It may sound small, but we are talking thousands of attempts, hours and hours. I knew there were never going to be any medals or cheers. The only person I had told or who could really see how far I had come was my mum. If I'd said to my mates, 'I walked up the stairs without holding on today', they'd have been like, cool, well done, mate. But they couldn't see what that really meant. It was so bloody difficult. *So bloody difficult.* Mum's reaction of joy and happiness for me when she saw me achieving something that is so small for able-bodied people, but absolutely ginormous for me, just kept me pushing forward. She's always said that she wasn't surprised to see me walking more again, partly because I did walk a lot more in front of her at home (as otherwise she would have had me stretching all evening) and partly because she says she knew how determined I was. But she knew what I'd had to put myself through and was just so proud of me for getting there.

PHYSICAL AND MENTAL STRENGTH ARE PART AND PARCEL

Going through these exercises built me up from the outside inwards – the confidence I was gaining back in my body was spilling over into my self-esteem. I knew my limitations in certain areas, so as soon as I had mastered one aspect of my mobility, I would turn my focus there. Once I felt totally comfortable at school, it was time to take it further afield and I challenged myself to move around London on my own. I duly fell over on cobbled streets, but cut hands can be wrapped up and I just got on with it. The next phase was really learning to stretch my pain barrier. It is simply a fact that my legs will hurt after a certain amount of exertion, so it became a question of how long I could go without sitting down. Could I manage the discomfort for 15 extra minutes? Then half an hour? Then an hour?

Building my physical strength was tied fundamentally to building my mental strength. For me, I cannot see the distinction between the two, because without working on a shatterproof mentality there was no way I could have built myself physically. Absolutely no way. Equally, the physical progress I made bolstered my mental strength, in this kind of self-perpetuating loop. The easier it was to walk, the easier it was to push myself until I stopped even seeing it as hard. Of course, it was never easy. I will never again in my life have a day as physically easy as it was when I was in my chair. I will be in pain to a greater or lesser extent every single day I am on this Earth. Those are the cards I have been dealt. But now I know I would prefer to battle that than the alternative. It is way less painful to me to have tender muscles than to know I'm letting myself down.

Once I had really reached a solid place with my walking, I turned my attention back to doing sport. I decided to start with basketball because I have good hand-to-eye coordination. I could never get to where I needed to be fast enough, but if I was ever close to the hoop, I would always score. But even running around to that limited extent, using my legs and pushing through the barrier, made a dramatic difference. Every morning after practice or a game, I would wake up to throbbing legs, totally dead. But I knew it was a good thing. These days, I swim a lot, because the pain-to-progress ratio of other forms of exercise isn't worth it for me any more. I'm strong enough to drive my race car and do whatever it is I need to do. I can get anywhere independently on my own two legs, so I don't need to do that level of training any more. It just depletes me and has more of a negative impact on my joints and skeleton as a whole now. But back then, I needed to keep stepping things up to get to where I wanted to be.

The strength I found through this time all came from my parents and the philosophy they had raised me with. Tough love sounds really cliched, but that is what it was. There was never a minute when I didn't know how much my parents cared for me and they were never ever cruel or unkind to me. My mum is such a softie, just an amazing woman who loves me to bits. I wouldn't be half the man I am today without her. But she also doesn't let me get away with anything. She was constantly on my case. 'Nic, straighten your legs!' Even when I said to her, 'I can't', she would say, 'Well, try!' She never, ever said, 'Ahh, never mind, if you can't do it, then that's OK.' Me saying that I 'couldn't' was not an option for my mum, which she continued to drum into me. She knew that it was all preparation for when she wouldn't be there.

There were definitely times when it would have been so easy for them to have made things simpler for me. They could have helped me up the stairs at home, they could have done everything for me, like served me all my drinks and food. These things can be hugely challenging when you struggle with balance and coordination. I 100 per cent resented their hard-line attitude at times and I wasn't always exactly thrilled with their approach. Sometimes I would be really angry with them, as certain things felt so unfair in the moment. Why can't you just help me and make this easier for me? But they never would. However, any of that resentment has turned into gratitude in my adult life, because I know how incredibly valuable my mentality has been in shaping my life, opportunities and expectations. Without them I would be living half the life I am today.

Building from my experience getting out of my wheelchair, I am now extremely wary of anything that looks or feels like the easy route. With maturity and earned wisdom, I can now identify that the hardest way is generally the one which leads you in the right direction. The harder route has always led me to personal growth and got me closer to what I want in life. If there is an opportunity to do better or challenge myself further, but it's a harder direction, that is my path. I am not looking for convenience or ease. I'm looking for the route to achievement. The easy way is often easy *now* but leads to difficulties later on – it's basically a con. This is a learning I want to share with everyone, because I truly believe it has value, on a daily basis, to transform the way we all live our lives.

You don't have to give me any excuses or explain the appeal of the easy route. I know it all! I have been there! I loved it in the moment, too. I often speak to people living with the exact same challenges as me and I do find it hard to know that they are living less of a life than they need to be. Knowing people who physically *can't* do it and would desperately give *anything* to have the chance of mobility always motivates me even more to persuade others who could to give it a try. If you can do something – as in, it is physically available to you – at least have a go. Of course, I also try to have compassion and give people grace, because we were all raised differently and our experience of any kind of condition will inevitably be different. But now I've been through the valley and come out the other side, I try to inspire others to defy the odds too.

Recently I visited a specialist school for kids living with CP and I met an incredible eight-year-old girl who had exactly the same version of the condition as me. She stood there, wearing splints that would slide into her shoes for ankle support, her knees bent and standing on her tiptoes. I was basically looking at an eight-year-old version of myself. Her task for the day was to walk up a flight of stairs, get to the top, turn around and walk back down. Sounds easy, doesn't it? Well, not for an eight-year-old with CP. Her range of movement was so limited that just making the effort to pick up her right leg high enough to reach the first step took it out of her.

She had an amazing helper who would be egging her on for support, giving her the strength, but as I stood there, watching her, as a 30-year-old, fully unaided, no splints, no walking stick and now a range of movement and balance which meant I would be able to walk with ease up and down those steps she was struggling so hard with, big, fat tears started rolling down my cheeks. I couldn't help but feel both pride and sadness for her. Pride, because of her determination and mental resilience to keep pushing through the struggle, with no complaints, and sadness, because I just wanted to take the struggle away for her, as I knew that this was just the beginning.

But even though it was so difficult for her, she didn't lose hope, she just kept going. Only I knew what that really felt like, what it really meant. In that instant, I realized how hard it must have been for my parents, because all I wanted to do was help her. Scoop her up, hold her hand. Looking back, if I could just make it easier for her in that moment or put myself in that position, I would want to. What I have learned is that it takes more strength to step back than to ride in and help a person you love. By standing firm and always, *always* making me dig deep to find the strength within myself, my parents gave me the greatest gift of all.

Today, there are so many times when I think, God, just this once can I be lazy or take the easy route? But for some reason it's not there for me any more. Let's say we were playing a computer game and you played on a mode that was easier than was entirely necessary, so I felt I should too. I wouldn't feel any sense of achievement if I succeeded or completed the game at the lower level because I would know that I was cheating myself. I wouldn't be shouting from the rooftops about anything if I knew I hadn't really tried or pushed myself to what I was capable of. If someone tells me to do 10 reps, I have to do 15 or 20. I can't back out. My experiences have hardwired that into me, so it's not even a habit, more like an instinct. That doesn't mean that I'm strong everywhere or that parts of my mentality are invulnerable. I'm definitely not indestructible and I have my Achilles heels. But in certain parts of my mentality, I cannot be knocked down. It doesn't matter what you say or do.

If you are reflecting on some of your choices and know that you have dodged a harder route, I understand wholeheartedly how you have got there. Perhaps you are happy with where you are and feel no sense of discontent or longing for anything different. But if you have this niggling doubt or deep down know that you could have asked more of yourself, then maybe that first step really is to look at yourself very honestly and admit where maybe you let an obstacle beat you. When I turned 16, I thought about all the things I wanted for my life ahead. I knew I wanted to have a career and I really hoped that it would be in motorsport. I wanted to be accepted; I wanted to have relationships. I wanted to have the chance to experience the world. Did I have all of that? Did I have a route towards it? Definitely not. I didn't feel strong, or good about myself, or accepted. I felt crap within myself because I knew I wasn't fulfilling my potential and I had made my own life smaller for no other reason than I could not be bothered to get up and walk.

Once you reach a conclusion that the easy route is what has led to your unhappiness and discontentment, look it square in the face and acknowledge all the factors that led you there. Then say to yourself, I've taken this route, but I'm at the end of it today. It has served me to this point, perhaps in many ways. It could continue to serve me, but if I carry on down the same road, I'm not going to get to where I want to be.

NO EXCUSES, BUT PLENTY OF KINDNESS

We all know in the moment when we're taking the easy route. I personally get a feeling of restlessness and guilt. If you continue excusing yourself, there will be no progress. You can't expect change unless *you* change. The majority of the time, the change is not going to come to you, you're going to be the one who has to go out there and *make* the change. Another person can only help you up to a point and when you get there, it is only you who can continue striving onwards in your own direction. And besides, people will give up on you if you give up on yourself, which is something I have experienced first-hand. You have to be able to rely on yourself to forge ahead.

That doesn't mean that you have to push yourself to horrendous extremes every day. I know I should go to the gym and have a swim today. I'm not going to go because my body feels tired. I know how to balance out my need to maintain fitness and do what is best for my racing and the reality of my condition. But I feel a sense of awkwardness about not going, because I do know I could do it if push came to shove. Sometimes you deserve to give yourself compassion, too. I deserve some time off and down time because I have worked so incredibly hard over the years. It's down to me, doing what I feel is right – compassion isn't the easy road.

A lot of so-called bad decisions arise simply out of immaturity, lack of experience and being young. But you mature through experience and overcoming challenges. Going down the wrong path has a lot of value for your personal development and, as we know, success and failure are knitted together. You have to learn the lessons yourself. This goes back, once again, to parenting. So many parents try to take pain and strife away from their kids and ease the weight of their baggage these days. That is almost what parenting has become about. But from my point of view, parents need to let their children do what they need to do and to learn from their own mistakes. What I thought was the best decision – going into a wheelchair – I *still* think was the best decision for me and I don't regret it. If someone told me now that they were going into school and they had CP and struggled walking long distances, I would tell them to use a wheelchair. That was not the mistake I made. I would, however, say to them, do not use it at home. Use it as little as possible outside of school. In and around the wheelchair use, I would suggest they work to build and maintain strength and do a lot of physio. Perhaps once a week, leave the chair behind and walk, or walk for half of the day. The aim would be about building them up over time to being able to gain the strength not to need the wheelchair as much.

These were the pitfalls I succumbed to. But I'm a true believer that before you can succeed you have to learn how to fail, and you have to go through the difficult moments to build yourself as a character. Once you've been there, done that, got the T-shirt, you know how to deal with it again. That won't make you bulletproof, but the more you go through the difficult times, the more you build an armour against anything else that comes in the future. Admittedly, experiences like these are never fun. When you're going through them, it still feels rubbish and awful and you have that voice asking, 'When is it ever going to end?' It still feels like that for me now. But, inside, you know it will end, because you have seen it end before and you have come out the other side. When you get there, you think, OK, I made it again. Every time you get there, it adds to your strength.

You will never know how far you can go until you take your first step. I'm not going to pretend that it will be a laugh, or that things will end up going your way. I have no way of knowing that. You could get to step five along your path and fall all the way back down to step two. What's important is that you don't step off the ladder completely. That you don't get scared by the first fall and reach for an easier ladder. On a ski trip with friends, one of our party was skiing at a decent level but had got to a point where he needed to go steeper to improve, which he really wanted to do so he could ski with the larger group. It's my belief that the only way you're going to get better at things is by *having* to get better at them. With skiing, for example, if you don't learn to turn faster, you will go faster, potentially too fast, lose control and fall. You have to learn to go down steeper runs to be able to progress.

Our friend was progressing really well, but all of a sudden, he fell and split his lip open, and it scared him. That was the last time he went on the slopes that trip. I remember saying that the worst thing he could possibly do was not ski again. In situations like these, you have to get up, force yourself to get back on the same run and get it done, because otherwise you throw away all the progress you have made and become so scared of the fall that you never go any further. The fall is actually part of the progress and though it was understandable, it was a shame that he let it get the better of him, because he had made such amazing improvements. In my mind he had set an upper limit for himself so far below his true limits because of fear. But, as I always say, you have to go through the ringer. The falls and the tumbles can be indicators of moving forward *if* you embrace them when they inevitably show up rather than fear them. Because of my condition, I am covered in scars and bruises, both physically and metaphorically, through blips on the road to progress. I have scars in the middle of my face, on my forehead and on the top of my lip. You have to push your boundaries and limits and learn from them and now I hardly fall any more.

My parents raised me to never accept other people's perceptions of my limitations. Through this chapter, I have really wanted to help you identify some of the limits that others might have placed on you and think how you too might have embraced the path of least resistance. How has giving up on the tougher path in your past shaped your present? What would it take for you to change direction? How might taking control of your own trajectory empower you to live a completely different life? When it comes to disability, it is hard because so many different people are affected in so many different ways. Some people can't feed themselves or walk or talk or communicate. So, me saying, just get up and drive a touring car, obviously that is never going to make sense in every context. That's not my point. What I'm trying to say is, try to fulfil your life to the edges of your potential, no matter what your abilities might be. Take control in every single way that you can. Work hard, push yourself and live for yourself, not how you might be perceived or what you have been told you can do or who you can be.

WITHIN YOUR LIMITATIONS, PUSH YOURSELF TO THE VERY EDGE

In addition to my mobility prognosis, doctors told my parents that my lazy eye would deteriorate over time and could potentially lead to blindness. As a racing driver I have yearly medicals and currently, in my early thirties, have 6:6 in both eyes. That's the benchmark for 'normal' vision. Not everything that you are told to expect will come to pass, which is one of the reasons I don't worry too much about anything medical. I try to live with my condition in the here and now. Lots of my friends don't even see my condition for what it is any more. A prime example was last time a group of us went to the cinema. I had my hands loaded up with popcorn and a drink and sweets, and cinemas are tough anyway because there often aren't rails to help you get up and down to your seat. All my friends went ahead, and I had to call for them. 'Hey, bro, can someone take my popcorn!?' 'Oh, shit, yeah!' one of them responded. 'I forgot you were wobbly!' The fact that people do forget is a sign of how far I have come.

Hearing other people's stories of accomplishment can be game-changing, but only if you allow it to be a game-changer. If you read what I'm saying and it resonates with you, that's great, but this is just my take – it isn't gospel. However, I do believe there are certain things you can take from other people's stories to help improve your life.

The fact that I exist means that there must be other people facing extraordinary challenges like me who could achieve amazing things. I want parents to know that it is possible, and I believe every child has the chance of being an outlier in some way, someone whose destiny doesn't lie in being 'average'. Every child can be the underdog turned hero. And that isn't through racing cars or running a business or anything specific. It's about exceeding people's perceptions and never stopping to reach for the stars. People love to see others fighting, giving it their all and their best. I am proud of so many people – especially the ones struggling but still smiling and fighting every day. People I know who have learned to live and build their lives in such extremely challenging circumstances and flourish even in physically extreme environments. They are the *true* heroes. Have they won races? No, but they are winning at their own life. Winning at your own life is all you can wish for. You can't win at someone else's life. It doesn't matter which car the person next to you is driving. All you can do is the best you can and find acceptance and contentment.

I have won at my own life (the only context that really matters) because I can do literally everything I want to do now. Before, I couldn't even go to the supermarket and get a pint of milk. Today I can overcome anything that comes my way. Icy pavements, slippery floors or steps with no handrails. If I decided I wanted to fly to Australia and travel around on my own, I could do that, no issues. Every single day I walk along feeling the privilege of what I have achieved. I don't agree with absolutely everything in terms of the way my parents raised me. If I ever become a father, there will be things that I will do differently. I don't condone every single element of their philosophy, but that is natural between generations anyway. Parents can't be perfect and it's impossible for them to get it right on every count. But I am in awe of the strength they found within themselves to bring me up this way. Everything I do in my life is a reflection of them, I'm a testament to them. Any time I jump in a race car and inspire people or stand up in front of thousands of people and share my story or write my own book, this book, it's all down to them. I hope when my parents look at Lewis and me they feel a huge sense of achievement. I hope they know how much they have given us both. It's something I hope I can share with everyone who reads this book, too.

Takeaways

* No one else can define your upper limits. They can't stamp you with rubber, nor can they ever truly know what you are capable of. Stats, case studies, sweeping surveys of people like you . . . they are not you. You are not an average, in fact there is always the chance you are an outlier. Remember that every single day it is only you who can push against your limitations and stretch what is possible in your own life.
* It is very easy to talk about change, but very difficult to do anything about it. I always say judge a person by their actions, not their words, and that is the standard I hold myself to. I didn't go on about getting out of my chair; once I'd made the decision, I started the long process to building my strength step by step. I'm not saying, 'Suffer in silence', more, 'Direct your energy and headspace to where they are most valuable – the actually doing, not the saying you'll do.'
* Self-compassion isn't the easy road; it is what will make achieving hard things over a period of time sustainable. Brutalizing yourself without ever giving

yourself the moment to take stock and appreciate how far you have come is like only using a stick and not a carrot to motivate yourself. Why not use every tool you have? Take breaks, take comfort, take support when you need it. While it is only you who can make these changes for yourself, it's not the suffering Olympics.

LESSON THREE

YOUR BULLIES ARE YOUR BEST MOTIVATORS

Bullying. At some stage in all of our lives, we'll have encountered a bully – whether that's at school, a tough kid in our local area, a terrible boss or nowadays online. When it's so easy to drop a horrible comment or pile onto someone online, it's no big surprise that it's become so commonplace. But bullying IRL is still rife – at least 20 per cent of schoolkids report being bullied in person. Having to confront emotional aggression and the worst side of human intimidation may, to some people, be considered a rite of passage, but just because it can be normalized doesn't mean that it can't wreak long-lasting damage on you and how you feel about yourself. In turn that can have a huge impact on your future and your ability to find the mental strength you need to achieve your dreams. I personally found that bullying planted a seed in my mind, a seed which grew into a weed, curling around my confidence and dragging me down, many years after the words were said or the physical acts committed.

I'll never forget back at school this kid telling me that I walked like I was in the mafia and couldn't even manage a straight line, then laughing at me and ridiculing me in front of a whole group of people because of it. Other kids would mimic the way I walked, just generally piss-taking, and that made me really aware that it was something which marked me out and drew attention. It can still happen now – I was walking out of the supermarket to my car during lockdown and these two kids walked past my car, mimicking my movements. They were with both of their parents and they all looked at me and the parents laughed at their kids' impression. The attention that my style of walking attracts is something which has never left me. Nowadays, I find it more annoying than embarrassing. I'm over it. I'm over the struggle, it doesn't reach my heart. But I am aware that it creates a conversation and can be something to make a joke about. You know when you get up from a table in a restaurant and you're walking through a crowd of people? I know in that moment there will probably be a kid there who has noticed the way I walk and they will point at me or ask questions about me loudly. In that moment it does make me uncomfortable. I don't care what they laugh about or what people think of me, but I do feel anxious in that moment because it brings back memories of bullies at school. If I'm honest, it mostly feels awkward to me.

Even now, bullies still target me on a daily basis. The online trolling and abuse I receive simply because of my condition are relentless. While I'm now confident in myself and have a really solid mental outlook, if you stand in the rain for too long, you're going to get wet. I'm not going to sit here and say that I've reached some higher level where it doesn't affect me at all any more. I actually don't believe that is possible. As humans, we are hardwired to seek approval and while you can absolutely train yourself to tune out that noise and find your inner voice, dealing with pointed negativity from others is always going to leave some kind of mark. So instead of saying, 'Learn to rise above it' or 'Let it be water off a duck's back', the lesson I want to impart in this chapter is about shifting the way you deal with bullies and reconsidering how you see the bullies themselves.

It is a sad fact of life that there are going to be people in the world who interpret your vulnerabilities, whatever they may be, as weakness, and see demeaning you as an opportunity to build their own self-esteem. There is so much trauma in circulation, with so many people who have been through or are going through difficult and triggering experiences that remain entirely unresolved. I have had years of therapy and a huge amount of mental health support which have helped me process my own issues and experiences. But that is a privilege. I have learned that there are lots of people out there sitting in deep pain. My bullies or trolls are clearly not in a great place. Taking pot shots at me reveals their own inner demons. The words can sting, of course, but you have to try to contextualize everything in terms of where it's all coming from.

For me, my experiences with bullying began at school. In so many ways, I have been fortunate. My parents sheltered and shielded me from a lot of shit going on in the world, especially when it came to my race and abilities. They did an amazing job of protecting me, so much so that as a young kid, I didn't even know that Black and mixed-race people were mistreated or treated in a different way from others. I didn't know that disabled people were victimized. I didn't know about the structural issues that people who lacked privilege were experiencing, and that shows my own advantages. I didn't know how the world perceived someone like me. So, when it came to school and being away from my parents' shelter, it was a bit of an awakening.

Even though I was in a minority of one, at primary school I wasn't bullied or anything like that. In the early weeks, the other kids initially stared and asked questions that I didn't have the answers to. I got laughed at and pointed at sometimes, but it fizzled out to, OK, we see that he is different, what can we do about it? Nothing. Young kids can be absolutely savage sometimes, simply because they haven't learned or experienced difference, but fortunately nothing ever escalated beyond that for me as a young boy.

Perhaps surprisingly, given everything I have overcome, I'm still quite insecure around children. When I'm at, say, a swimming pool and there are kids around, I know that I can present a challenging and even scary sight for them. If they haven't seen difference, or ever met a disabled person, I know that I can be alarming to them by the way I walk and my general movements. And I hate the idea that I am the person that triggers that for them, because I want to be a person who triggers security and love in people, especially in children. I want to make people feel comfortable. When they get to know me, kids love me. Once I get past that initial barrier, the connection always builds positively and they shed the fear. Sometimes they will want me to pick them up straight away and hold them, and I can't always do that unless I am either sitting down or have my back against something solid for support. It reassures me that kids can see through it and past it and that makes me believe that one day I will be a good father and my daughter or son will see *me*, not just my condition. But as someone who looks and is different, as much as it's great to be part of a teachable moment for young humans, it can also be tough to be around small kids.

On the playground back at school, children struggled to be friends with me because I was so different. They didn't know if I could come and play football and I couldn't really play tag or it or whatever it was, because I could never catch them. Sometimes kids would take advantage of that because they knew it was impossible for me. Some of them definitely enjoyed the uneven competition – for me it was like being piggy in the middle, just being a foot shorter than everyone else. But there was never anything really co-ordinated or consistent, just the drip, drip, drip of feeling different.

The real problems started at secondary school. Bullying is always about power and is almost always characterized by the targeting of those seen to be in a weaker position. From day one, for obvious reasons, I had a target on my back. Because I had lived so far away from my primary school, when it came to moving on at 11, I ended up not knowing a single other kid in my year and had to try to make friends again. I didn't have Ben next to me to open doors to my being accepted – now it was just me alone. But I had arrived on my first day feeling really excited and confident. My legs were loose and supple from all the physio I had been doing and that made me feel relaxed and calm, but almost immediately I realized what a different ball game I was now dealing with. Aside from my struggle to navigate the huge distances between my classes, I can just remember feeling so physically overwhelmed by the size and number of all the other kids. I'm a short man generally, even without bent legs which have cost me another few inches. Everyone was taller than me, and back then it felt like they were physically looming over me. I was the only person of colour in the entire school – again – and I was obviously struggling with my movement, which generated even more attention. It was a big thing for me to deal with, but all I could do was work with what I had and do the best job I could to make myself feel included and welcome.

Initially that was *really* difficult. Because, really, we were all still children. We weren't able to have mature, reasoned conversations about things like prejudice yet. From day one, I felt constant stares and whispering behind my back, which was obviously really awkward for me. I tried to make friends and speak to people in my form group, but hardly anyone was open to it. All the cool kids made it obvious that they were never going to accept me, and I did feel really bruised. It felt so unfair – if I hadn't been disabled, would they have been snickering at me? I ended up tagging along with a group of people who were seen as 'nerds'. They were never nerds, they were, and are, the most awesome people, but we were definitely a band of misfits.

PUSHING BACK AGAINST VICTIMIZATION

After a few months of feeling so intensely under the microscope, I decided it was probably best to face it head on. I asked my teachers if I could stand up in front of my whole year group in assembly and explain a little bit about my condition. I didn't tell my parents and all I asked my teachers for was a bit of time to speak to my year group, because I felt that a lot of my fellow students didn't understand what I was going through and why I walked differently and looked different. I guess at that time being stared at constantly had become too much for an 11-year-old to deal with.

My teachers were really supportive and, looking back, I suppose it was my first experience with public speaking. They just said, of course, we will give you all the time you need to say what you want to say. Even to this day, I never plan my speeches – what I say just comes from the heart. Back at school, that's what I did. I shared how I felt in that moment, and it was probably no longer than five minutes. I remember not really feeling nervous, just more hopeful that it would help change things. 'I'm Nic and I've got this condition. I don't know why I have it but let me tell you what I know about it.'

I went on to tell them as much as I understood about CP and ended by saying, 'Please don't stare at me so much now – if you have a question, just ask me and I'll answer it in the best way I can, but I'm still working through it all.' Looking back now, that moment was the moment my mum said would always come. The moment when I would be able to find strength in my vulnerability and see my unique circumstances as nothing to be ashamed of.

That was the first time I was able to stand up and talk about myself and confront everything I felt inside. All the mental issues and struggles that I was having. It actually propelled me to a new sense of confidence about it all and in retrospect I have realized that, more than doing it for other people, I did it for myself. I had told the teachers the talk was about introducing myself to everyone, because no one would give me the time of day on the playground, but I didn't do it for them. I did it for my own self-esteem and to force my presence around people where I had been excluded because of my condition. It was one of the first examples of my motto to turn up whether people like it or not, because that is what I've had to do my whole life. I have been ignored and sidelined and segregated and shut out of things so many times and, by age 12, I had already learned to push back against that.

Everyone did stop staring, for a while at least, though the response to my solo in assembly was quite muted – it wasn't like

I was some avenging hero or something; no one came to speak to me after the talk. It was more like people backed off because they understood more. It made them *less* interested, in a way. They knew why I looked and moved differently, so they didn't laugh or take the mick out of me as much, as they could see it for exactly what it was. After the bloody assembly moment, I then had to introduce the wheelchair, which was another reason to make me more conspicuous and different. But people got used to that too, after a while.

When I started using a wheelchair at school, it was a novelty, because no one had known anyone in a wheelchair before and everyone wanted to give it a go by pushing me here and there. But then as I grew older, developed and used my wheelchair for everything, the shine wore off. I do understand – there was so much for people to take in. I was a kid with CP, in a wheelchair, and I was mixed race. Of course, it drew attention. It must have been hard for them as well. Kids don't always think before they speak or act, but often it's not their fault either – they are learning too.

There's no denying that, in a school environment, being disabled is seen as deeply uncool in lots of ways. All the accessories look shit in my eyes. Splints aren't cool. Modified shoes aren't cool. There is very little to make a disabled person look cool factored into any design of the things we need to take part in society. We've got to have these trainers that are better for us to walk in, but they look like dodgy platform shoes. Disabled kids out there want to look cool and go to the club and wear the right sneakers and chains or whatever it is. They don't want to turn up in disabled clogs. So, of course, I ended up wearing normal sneakers which I knew were terrible for my feet, because I would rather feel comfortable in my own skin, by looking or feeling cool, and then deal with the physical consequences afterwards. I wouldn't say I am the best role model when it comes to this, but I did what made *me* feel good at the time and still does today.

KEEP YOUR FRIENDS CLOSE

For a couple of years things were OK for me. Over time I had made two best friends, Dan and Pete. Pete was a straight-A student and super smart in every way. He would turn up to school with his top button done right up, looking the smartest out of everyone, when all the so-called 'cool kids' at school were wearing their ties knotted differently and with their collars undone. He also had ginger hair and was bullied from time to time for being the way he was. Pete has become an amazing musician – he was always so talented. He now plays the bass and the bass guitar for loads of different artists. Then there was Dan, who has always been like an in-betweener. He was never nerdy, never the average cool kid, but he was *super cool* with his own style and personality. To me, he was just a decent dude and an incredible saxophonist. These two guys were so clever, and we were all obsessed with music, so I decided to start playing the drums and we formed a little band.

I often found I got on better with people in the years above me because they were more mature and more accepting. While I was singing in a school play, I met a guy from the year above playing the drums. His name was Phil, he wore glasses and I'm sure some saw him as a geek. But he was never a geek, just the most kind-hearted and warm person. Not to mention the best drummer I'd ever heard at that age: even now, he is incredible. I just wanted to be like him. Over time, he also became part of our friendship group and joined the band. A couple of girls joined as singers and we all basically lived in the music block. That was our thing and it really solidified proper friendships. By the time I was 15 and going into Year 11, one of the best people in my life, Alec, also joined our school. His uncle taught there and had always been my absolute favourite teacher. Alec is such a unique person, always full of positivity, jokes and laughter, but can be a voice of wisdom when it is asked of him. He is now a teacher, living in Dubai. Before long, Alec had become like Ben, and I felt like I had that proper support mechanism again.

All this is to say that my crew had become really tight and I was lucky enough to have people who really cared for me. The friends I made were awesome, smart, clever and kind. They were driven and passionate and accepting. Becoming friends with them really boosted me and made me feel secure. I didn't need to go anywhere else or be friends with anyone else, the four or five of us were happy as Larry together. We just tried as much as we could to keep ourselves to ourselves, but it is true that we were all to some extent victimized. What is cool or uncool at school rarely translates beyond the gates. Sure, a certain group of people saw us as losers. The people who were smoking cigarettes behind the skip, getting the girls and picking on kids in the year below. We just tried to avoid them and focused on our studies and our music. Even at that age, I realized that was far more aspirational. But my friends were not fighters. We were, and still are, lovers through and through. So, when a new phase began sometime after I turned 15, my friends could never have been there to protect me physically, nor would I have wanted them to be.

*

This new era had all started with 'jokes' at my expense, the kind of thing you're meant to take on the chin and laugh at to prove you don't take yourself too seriously. One afternoon, in the middle of the form room, this one boy approached me and held out a T-shirt he had produced with the word 'WHEELS' printed across it. To be clear, it wasn't an affectionate term: it referred to my wheelchair and he did it to humiliate me in front of the whole class. Then there was a booby cake that he and his friends thrust on to my lap for my birthday a few months later, laughing themselves to tears at the public shaming. Don't get me wrong, I *love* boobs now. If someone got me a booby cake today for my birthday, I would thank them and give them a high-five! However, back then, they made me a laughing stock. Then things turned more physical. This time, it was a different group of boys and whenever they saw me, they would band together to tip my wheelchair backwards so I would be stranded on my back, totally unable to move until someone came to help. At the time I didn't have the strength to get out from that position and they knew I would be trapped. They would always target me when there was no one around and it meant I started being late for classes because I would just be stuck there. I can't tell you how crushing it felt, knowing that I couldn't defend, or even really fend for, myself. Every day I knew I was a sitting duck and there was absolutely nothing I could do about it. That was really tough for a young kid to deal with, any young kid going through all the regular teenage stuff, but especially for one also dealing with my condition.

I always believed the best response was silence and I decided I would never give them the satisfaction of knowing they had got to me. But when you've been at the receiving end of this kind of thing, it can run really deep, even years down the line. Bullying isn't just in the moment; it can have a long-term impact on your self-esteem. It can hit at your very foundation. While the pain of bullying is usually felt most when we're teenagers, because our sensitivity to rejection is so heightened around that age, victimization can lead to feelings of shame, self-worthlessness, chronic depression and anxiety for the rest of our lives. While we often see it just as something that is par for the course, especially among lads, the whole 'boys being boys' rubbish, bullying can inform everything that comes after it. Turning that around has been a huge factor in strengthening my mentality. And for me it's operated in two ways – firstly empathy for those who bullied me and secondly finding self-confidence in proving the haters and doubters wrong.

But I'm getting ahead of myself. Before I reached any kind of clarity on the situation, I definitely thought I was in some part to blame for the attacks. And as usual when I had any issue, I went to my big brother to ask for his advice. What Lewis told me to do was to try to turn the story around. OK, so my wheelchair was the focus of the attention and there was no way I could do without it physically, so why not try to make it seem cool again? He suggested I become more of a daredevil in my chair, almost like the 'old school' skateboarder Tony Hawk, but in a wheelchair. Lewis taught me to do tricks – wheelies, bunny-hopping down the stairs and over obstacles and all that stuff. For about five minutes it did work. But then just as quickly it didn't.

At that point, I felt like I needed to change myself by getting the bullies' attention and making my chair appear novel and interesting in order to gain acceptance. For a beat I thought that was the only way to stop the bullying and find the validation I was seeking.

I now know it was the worst thing I could have done. The older I have grown, and the more I have learned about being the odd one out, the more I have realized that leaning into your difference and becoming comfortable with the quirks that make you is really the best defence against bullies. If you try to change yourself to escape the notice of people who feed off others' vulnerabilities, they will always be there at the back of your mind. If you are truly going to be yourself and live the best life you can, you have to do everything you possibly can to reject those messages of hate. In a similar way to pretending you're someone else on social media, trying to get the bullies to accept me by posting things that I thought might impress people or make them more interested in me was only taking me further from the person I really was and stopping me from accepting myself.

Over time, I have come to realize that the negativity I have experienced in my life has actually only spurred me on to success. I still sometimes think about my school bullies and how their attempts to belittle me only made me stronger and more determined. I don't mean that I sat down and thought, right, this is how I'm going to get my revenge on these arseholes, by making them realize that I am actually amazing, and they will regret how they treated me. It was more: let them say and do what they want, I'm going to be a success either way. I got on with my life and my studies, and I ended up getting out of my wheelchair. That was one way of stopping them humiliating me and, although I was short, I was pretty ripped for a 16-year-old, the result of pushing myself around for years and constantly using my arms in general movement. Strangely, when I stood on my own two feet, they weren't so confident at pushing me over.

THROUGH THE EYES OF A BULLY

Thanks to that process of building my physical strength, I became stronger emotionally and could see that it was my mates who were the cool people, the ones we'd all like to be around. They never made me feel that my wheelchair was uncool, and it was always OK to be different, because my mates always accepted me for who I was. Every day, I went to school and I learned more and more that the bullies are the kids in detention who you don't want to mix with. They're always trying to make you feel like *you're* in a bad place when, even with the smallest amount of perspective, it's clear that *they* are the ones in a bad place. Bullies hurt people, but the person they hurt the most is themselves. Most bullies will have a downward spiral in their life as their bullying impacts their learning, their relationships and their professional life. It is a terrible thing to be a bully, because it shows an absolute lack of ability to relate to other people. I feel a deep sympathy for them: the people who bullied me at school might never find contentment, success or happiness because they are damaged in a way that is very difficult to come back from. If someone is targeting a disabled kid in their class, I think we can all agree things can't be going that well in their life. Whether that's their fault or not, bullying a disabled kid in a wheelchair can be considered the lowest of the low. It's not exactly #goals, is it?

As life has gone on, I've grown more interested in the complexities of mental health and become more educated and gained more empathy through my own battles. Overcoming elements of my own mind and getting to grips with how the experiences of bullying and exclusion undermined my confidence and self-belief through professional therapy have led me to understand how so many others, including my bullies, struggle themselves. It may not be their fault – it may be how they were brought up or the circumstances of their childhood. Or they may just be going through a difficult time. I began to not judge people by the way they reacted to me and have tried to understand them in terms of their reactions – because there can be so many layers to any individual's lens. Some people might shout at you but, if you give them a hug, they will embrace you. It took me a long time to see the bigger picture and that has made me have empathy for my bullies. I'm now at the point where I actually want to find the guys who gave me the most grief at school and ask them how it's going. I don't hold resentment or hatred; I have released all of those feelings now.

My schooldays were an intense period of personal growth. The experiences I navigated there made me realize that I didn't have to be a certain way, I just had to be *me*, in whatever way I wanted to be. If I had just been accepted by everyone and had never been targeted, I wouldn't have had that space for growth. I now see that I was actually being accepted in the right places and being pushed in the right direction. If the bullies and cool kids had welcomed me in, I might have ended up on the wrong path, smoking and drinking behind the skip with them too, late for school and skipping classes. Maybe I would have become a rebel in that direction because that's what they said was cool; perhaps I would have never regained my focus. I mean my dad would have killed me first, obviously. But what I realized was that sometimes when you think you want to be accepted in one place and you're not, it can be really gutting. Then, as time goes on, you realize you weren't accepted for a reason.

I've gone down a completely different path in my life, not just because of the amazing friends I made but also because of the terrible friends I didn't make. School taught me everything about perceptions. Some people will like you, some won't. Some will think you're cool, others won't. It's mostly all to do with them and very little to do with you. It could be your colour, or because you got a better grade than them. It could be because someone else likes you or said something mean behind your back. It could be because they are so completely disempowered at home and treated so badly that they need to dominate you to claw back their own self-esteem. You can't know the web of reasons why other people feel certain ways about you, so you just have to be *you*.

I carried what I learned into my life after school and I just wanted to be me. Yes, I was different, but *whatever*. I'd got this far, I had friends. I'd survived some hard experiences, so bring it on. What I hadn't factored in was how social media and the internet were going to change things so dramatically.

NAVIGATING BULLYING IN ADULTHOOD

In real life, I am one of the most universally liked drivers on the BTCC grid, but from the outside, I am probably the most *disliked*. The amount of shit I get online is just out of control: for someone who had never experienced this kind of thing, it would be unbelievable. The internet has turbocharged all of the issues we've been exploring in this chapter. Anonymity has been shown to lead to much more aggression and lack of compassion among bullies and there is the sense that the negative social consequences of bullying have been stripped away by the facelessness of the web. The sheer intensity of the trolling is frankly depressing and sometimes I really wish I had stayed ignorant about the level of negativity out there.

When I announced my first season in motorsport, I was pretty oblivious as to how widespread trolling and cyberbullying were. I knew they existed, of course, and had seen Lewis go through some issues with them, but I was just not prepared for how much of a target my disability, and to a lesser extent my race, would make me. The hate started on day one. Day one! In my mind I was just a kid who wanted to race. Going into it all, I didn't realize the publicity I was going to have right from the beginning, nor that, no matter what, no matter how lovely and kind you might be, or how difficult or even tragic your circumstances, with publicity in this day and age comes negativity. Immediately I started receiving this barrage of tweets and messages. It would be people posting horrendous comments about my appearance and abilities, terrible things about my family or just about disability in general. When I started making my first mistakes – of course there were going to be mistakes, I was literally practising at the races, after all – I became the easy target again. I would love to say that all my experiences at school meant it didn't get to me, but it did. Actually, over time, it really ground me down and with every season it got worse.

Even to this day, I continue to get the most criticism online out of all the drivers on the BTCC grid. I understand that I am a particularly appealing target for a troll. I appear weak because of my disability, but I'm also privileged because of my family and connections, and that pisses people off. I'm mixed race, but also very successful on several stages. If you don't like Lewis or my dad, you won't like me. You've made your decision. If you believe that I'm only here because of Lewis's money, you've made your decision.

If you don't believe in my determination or my talent, or else my determination and talent make you feel inadequate, you've made your decision. However much I progressed, however hard I worked and however much my team believed in me, it could never change what the keyboard warriors wrote about me, because to acknowledge those things would have disrupted their unkind narrative.

We would all love to believe that our fellow human beings want the best for us. But I know that, in too many cases to count, this is just not true. A lot of the grief stems from the fact that I haven't won a race and that the majority of the time I'm nearer the back of the field. But in most instances, I'm only a few tenths of a second off the pace, for God's sake. Considering everything else I'm dealing with, it does seem unusual that I receive so much vitriol in comparison to other drivers in similar positions. But you know, they don't want to hear a story of resilience or of overcoming strife. They just want to see me fail. At the end of the day, I've never wanted people to treat me any differently, and trolls are unfortunately part of a successful sporting career. So, I don't bemoan the fact that I get attacked. What enrages me is how much more intense the attacks are on people with marginalized identities when they are already so overburdened. It's already a totally unfair playing field and yet our digital culture seeks to double down on discrimination and capitalize even further on any kind of perceived vulnerability.

Earlier in my career, the kinds of things that really got to me were comments about how I didn't deserve to be on the grid. It would be things like 'I hope the team have plenty of spare parts and an unlimited budget' or 'I bet he won't make turn one' or 'Year in, year out, what a waste of a seat on this guy'.

When you read something like that, there is part of you deep down inside that maybe believes an element of it to be true, and it makes your heart sink into your boots. That's how it was for me, at least. And you can become obsessed with it. I became fixated with reading negative comments about myself. I found myself looking and looking and looking. Scrolling past all the positive comments, compulsively seeking out the negative ones. Even though there were so many more positive ones than negative. The positive probably outnumbered the negative ones by a factor of ten. But reading the positive ones never made me feel any better. When you get to the stage where you truly believe, fuck, people hate me and maybe I am terrible – especially if you aren't sharing your experiences with the people around you or a professional – you can reach a really dark and lonely place. If someone said, wow, you're amazing, or what you're doing is incredible, that might boost me maybe 1 per cent. But then when I read a negative comment it would knock me down by 60 per cent.

The person I turned to during that time was Lewis again, because he has been there and done that. In fact, if he hadn't managed his experience, he would still be there now, because the hate doesn't take a day off. When I confided in him about what I was going through, he just told me, don't read *anything*. At the beginning he read both the good and the bad and he told me how difficult that experience had been for him, even though he is so incredibly strong mentally and arguably the most successful and talented driver in motorsport history. He too went through times of tough comments and digital bullying and still does today. His biggest takeaway is that anything that can impact your mind can impact your racing, so you have to protect yourself. He also told me that you have to give up the positive comments too. You can't have one without the other and what I've realized is that neither of them matter or add value to your life. Because it's all external validation. Of course, it's nice that people see me for what I am and want to support me. But at the end of the day, I'm doing it for me. I don't want to let either side overtake me. I'm the one hustling. I'm the guy doing it. Steering the whole direction of where I am going. Grafting daily to gain sponsorship and funding to get on the grid in the first place, overcoming my condition, doing my workouts, staying on top of my physiotherapy, designing my helmet and race suit. *I'm* the guy doing it all: I only need my own feedback, regardless of what people say or think.

As time has gone on, I've realized that you can't control anyone else's perception of reality *and* that people base their understanding of others on tiny shreds of information. The lengths people will go to to be negative are often irrational and astounding. When I drive past people at 150mph – and I might be having a bad race and be sitting fourth to last – I'm still doing an *amazing* job. Just think, I was in a wheelchair 15 years ago, unable to walk, and here I am, competing with and *beating* 'top' able-bodied touring-car drivers. Anyone out there behind a laptop or in the crowd who wants to try to drive as fast as me, with my condition and the limitations I have, give it a go and *then* let *me* judge *you*. People are so easy and fast to judge. I get so much of 'He's only there because of Lewis, or his dad' or 'He's only there because he's disabled, or Black', or whatever they want to say. I *know* the amount of effort and work that have gone on physically and mentally for me to drive past you at 150mph, racing able-bodied people. I do not have to place value on your judgements, because they mean nothing to me.

In 2023, I posted my first video on TikTok, just to try it. It went viral and got 3.4 million views, which completely shocked me. I wrote a short message about how doctors told me I wouldn't ever be able to walk and shared some footage of me walking in my race suit and helmet. Being new to the platform, I decided to see what kind of feedback was out there and if anything had changed – considering it was such an objectively positive message. The comments were savage. 'In what world is *this* classed as walking?' 'That's not walking where I come from.' 'Lol, I thought he was drunk, pathetic.' I could have just sat there and read them all coming in one after another and let them bury me in hate, but I remembered Lewis's advice. It is so important to remember that if we didn't have social media, those messages would have never touched me, they wouldn't have reached my eyes. But they have and it's something I have had to learn to deal with. I stopped reading almost immediately and stepped away. Even though I had an understanding that it could be a toxic environment, I'm also always under pressure to be present in some way, so I can't just fully disengage. But I can absolutely unplug from the negativity.

I wanted to share these experiences with you because I know that it's not just people like me, people vaguely in the public eye, who receive this kind of negativity online. Trolling is endemic, especially if you are disabled, or a person of colour, or from another marginalized group. Just by existing you can provoke people. It can be incredibly embarrassing to admit that these words have got to you or overtaken all the positive messaging. Lots of us like to think we're tough and can cope with criticism, but trolling cuts in a different way. We all need to feel OK about talking about it and admit that it can be thorny. There aren't easy answers.

I experimented with different approaches before I came to the conclusion that I shouldn't read anything. In the past I even reached out to my trolls to see if they were OK. Some of the exchanges were fairly positive, but, you know, I'm not a therapist. I can't put all my energy into helping people deal with their mental health issues, because I would never be able to achieve my own goals. I also have to be really careful about what I say publicly, because even though someone could have been mercilessly targeting me for months, telling me, 'You're shit, you're shit, you're shit', I can't turn around and say, 'Oh right, I'm shit, am I, so how's your life going, mate?' People would be like, fucking hell, that Nic Hamilton is a horrible human. I have to respond to negative comments very carefully as, in my position, I'm held to a higher standard and have teams, sponsors and management relying on me. You can throw as many stones at me as you want, but if I throw a *rock* back, people forget my smashed house. It's all 'Lewis Hamilton's brother Nic is such an arsehole.' I have to respond in a way that sticks up for myself, but not in a way that disrespects someone else, even if they have disrespected me. It's impossible to achieve that balance, so that's another reason I prefer to cut off their oxygen by not looking at all.

In many ways I find comments about my condition easier to swallow because I am entirely secure with it. When it comes to my racing, it is definitely harder, because I am sometimes very hard on myself about results, so the comments can echo some of the things I say to myself. When I read negative comments, it can physically feel like being punched in the stomach. So, when it comes to dealing with it, I think we have to be honest and say that there is no perfect shield. But you can get better at coping and I want to share some of the ways I have learned to do that.

Firstly, as outlined above, I have limited what I read on social media these days and I think that is something that everyone should consider. I've realized through Lewis that it doesn't matter what you achieve, there will always be someone out there desperate to tear you down and tell you that you don't deserve it. My family receives so much online grief – some of it, especially when it comes to my dad and Lewis, is blatantly racist and there are a lot of people in this world who struggle to accept Black and mixed-race people succeeding. I don't actually have to deal with much of that – my experience of being disabled is that people don't see any other part of my identity – but seeing that shit all play out online has also made me really wary of wasting too much of my energy there. Obviously, not everyone is receiving negativity all day long, but you may still see a lot of it in comments under other people's profiles or on news sites, and over time that can be really poisonous as it makes you feel everyone is just tearing everyone else down. I always suggest trying to curate the content you consume online by being very considered about who and what you follow. If there is any prejudice, racism, misogyny or just general nasty opinions, simply unfollow and avoid. Don't be sucked down into the rabbit hole of reading it all – no good can ever come of it.

And secondly, as I managed to do with my schoolyard bullies, I have also been able to find a level of compassion for my online trolls. Anyone out there targeting someone vulnerable is showing us that they are struggling in some way. It is never about the target. They could be in a negative or depressive situation which no one else might know about. They could be sat in a dark room, feeling super lonely. They might be struggling to get out of bed. I have been in that place and while I never personally targeted others, I can see why they might feel the need to. I feel desperately sorry for those people and would love to help them believe they can turn their lives around too. Reframing the power dynamic and considering why these people are sending these awful messages can really help to come to terms with them.

On the positive side, I have built a wonderful, incredibly engaged online community – one part of which is my Discord community, XEEDX, which stands for Exceed Expectations that provides a non-judgemental space online for people to be themselves. The things that have drawn my community in are my honesty and humour – because I am being completely myself. A group of my followers from all over the world – USA, Germany, India and beyond – came to see my last race at Silverstone and building friendships there for myself and creating a space for other people to make friendships have really shown me the positive power of the internet, if it's used in the correct way. Just as it was for me at school, building true friendships is one way to mentally protect yourself from bullies. I'm not talking about making friends who will physically stand up to bullies for you – more friends who help remind you that your bullies' words are just words and don't come from a place of truth. That true acceptance for exactly who you are does exist, even online. You just have to find the right space for yourself, foster a community of people who share your values and outlooks, and protect yourself anywhere where negativity ferments.

When it comes to choosing friends, it is all about letting a relationship build. Life has taught me that I need to be around the right people, those who lift me up. And building those friendships can take time. I've had failures as well as successes on that front. It is very easy to let negative people into your life, just as it is easy to let negative messages dominate your field of view. See people for what they really are and be straight with yourself about that. It is all too easy to sugar-coat people's actions and pretend they are the people we wish they were.

I can count my friends on one hand, and I am absolutely OK with that. Since I've been able to enjoy a level of success and become well known in some circles, I'm often hit up by people from the past, trying to connect. That definitely grinds my gears! All of a sudden, these people are coming out of the woodwork? 'It was amazing going to school with you . . .' What do you mean? You never helped me! We didn't know anything about each other. Some of them even made my life hell.

As for motorsport, I don't have lots of close friends in the industry. Like all highly competitive sports, it's very rarely cosy. I absolutely give kudos to the motorsport industry for giving me the chance to race. Not just the MSA, but team managers from the Clio Cup Championship, where I made my debut in motorsport. The owners of the teams. The drivers themselves. No one kicked up a fuss or singled me out as a liability. Things could have been very different. But obviously when you're on the track it's not all warm and fuzzy. I keep myself to myself. I talk to my teammates, of course, and one other driver perhaps that I'm actually close with. But everyone else . . . I don't engage with too much. You can't trust anyone too far, that's just the nature of competitive sport. There have absolutely been times when other drivers have made me feel low and said something which undermined my confidence. We are literally at war with each other. I guess for a long time there was no professional respect, because in our sport – as in most sports – respect has always been based on speed and results. The first time

I felt like my peers really understood me and the magnitude of what I was achieving was the year my title sponsor pulled out right at the last minute. It was so close to the start of the season that there were question marks over whether I'd be on the grid at all, but I ended up getting there through dogged determination – a story I will go into in more length later in the book.

After this huge blow I ended up doing a speech in front of the whole grid and explained that I race for completely different reasons to them. For me, it is about changing the face of motorsport and how we see disabled people in our culture and in society in general. I spoke about my other career, inspiring people through public speaking around the world to overcome obstacles, and how my specific experience with motorsport was the perfect example of what you really can achieve with determination. I explained why and what I struggle with in the car and was just super honest about my condition and how it affected my racing. It seemed to hit a chord with a lot of drivers and there has been a change in attitude. If I were to message any of them and say, hey, man, could you help with this or that, they would give me time now. I don't need to be their friend, but I respect them all as drivers as I know how much it takes to be there. There are some drivers on the grid whose ability I am almost in awe of. Do I want to have dinner with them? Probably not. But you can still look up to someone and respect them massively. I'm not sure if that respect is always shared back to me, but I think some people can see that what I'm doing is about a bigger picture.

Occasionally, with bullies, you will get the chance to savour sweet moments and to feel a level of redemption and vindication. It's not always the case, but sometimes it does all come back around for you. After years of receiving these horrendous messages about my performances on the track, it would have been easy to resign myself to believing what they said about me and let it impact my motivation to keep pushing for results. Instead, I've continued to find optimism and hope. For the first race of the 2023 season, I arrived at the track feeling a little apprehensive. Donington Park isn't one of my favourite circuits and unusually, as my parents can't make every race, my entire family were there – Lewis hadn't been trackside since round one of the 2019 season, but he had turned up to surprise me. My team wasn't sure how it was going to go, as we hadn't done a lot of pre-season testing or preparation, so we were really behind the curve. It was just like, let's see what we can do. I'd almost written off the first round and planned to treat it as a practice.

As expected, we qualified near the back and I started twenty-first out of twenty-seven. As we were sitting on the grid, waiting to start our formation lap, it began to rain. My engineer had looked at the forecast and decided to take the punt, a gamble to go on wet tyres. So, we started from the pit lane, right at the back of the field. As soon as the race started, the rain began to get heavier and heavier. Aside from two other drivers who had had a similar idea, the rest of the field was on dry (slick) tyres and by the end of lap one, we were up to fifteenth. Unfortunately, the safety car* came out at the start of lap two, which bunched the pack up and meant that those who didn't manage to pit for wet tyres now had the opportunity to do so, which minimized the impact of my 'tyre gamble'. I was thinking

* The safety car is a physical vehicle, which is brought onto the track to limit the speed of the competing cars. It drives at a specific speed so that marshals can come out and rectify anything unsafe.

to myself, 'Oh no! I do not have the pace to continue to move forward if everyone behind me is on wet tyres too.'

Surprisingly, I did have the pace. Good pace, and I continued to make my way through the pack, overtaking those who were still on slick tyres and pushing on with those on wet tyres. I couldn't believe how well I was doing! I ended up coming through the pack and was running as high as fourth at one point. Bearing in mind that my best result up until this point was fifteenth, back in 2020, running in fourth was a totally foreign experience. The pressure was *huge*, I could so easily have blown the opportunity. If this had been three years ago, I may well have crumbled, but this is what experience gives you, I just drove *out of my skin* and ended up finishing sixth, which I have decided is the biggest achievement of my life to date.

When I came across the line and the team told me over the radio that I had finished sixth, I punched the air with joy and passion and screamed, 'Let's fucking *goooo!*' Then, a sense of calm came over me, almost as if what I had just achieved was what I expected of myself. Like, yeah, that is what I am here to do, race and get good results, I always knew I could do it.

However, when I came into the pit lane, and everyone was there screaming and jumping up and down with elation, all my emotions came out. I'd been dreaming of this moment for eight years and I had always been thinking about what I would do if I got a result that I was proud of in a race. When it actually came, I didn't realize how much emotion I was carrying. When you get into the pit lane and park outside of your garage, in the BTCC, you have to stay in the car for a minute or so to cool it down before you get out and I found myself just crying my eyes out, like howling crying. It was happiness, yes, but mainly it was the pain and relief for everything I'd gone through in my life. Reliving every time people had directed their frustrations towards me in the form of bullying or told me I was never going to achieve anything or be good enough. That I needed to get a different job, that I was wasting my time, that no one would ever sponsor me, that I'd never get the result. That included my own family from time to time. I have been so isolated for so much of my career, but finally, after sticking to my guns and pouring my whole life and life savings into motorsport because I believed in myself, it had all come good.

There wasn't a dry eye in the paddock. Mum was bawling, Dad was the proudest I had ever seen him. The number of messages and phone calls I received that night from other drivers, saying they were honoured to be on the grid with me and that I was creating history and they were proud to be a part of it, was insane. Lewis had been watching from the sidelines, quite a way from the pit lane, so unfortunately he was the only person missing in my 'pit-lane celebrations'. However, he contacted me a while later, congratulating me with passionate words and pride. He was just super excited for me. He said my driving was so awesome – and for him to say that meant the world to me. It felt like there was a reason they were all there, like it was fate or the universe sending me a message.

I still have an ambition to achieve a podium finish and to this day I believe that if that safety car hadn't come out on lap two, it would have been within my grasp. But really, this result was enough. I have proven everything I ever needed to prove – I'm a disabled man competing in an able-bodied sport and I managed to get that result. It took a while for that to sink in.

This achievement means so much to me, because when we're talking about bullying, so much of it is shielding yourself from other people's opinions, driving ahead and defining yourself on your own terms outside of that negativity. All of a sudden, perceptions of me and my career have flipped. Journalists and broadcasters from across the globe pushed this result hard on social media, and I was asked to do lots of interviews – even at my brother's next race, journalists asked him about *my result*. The magnitude of my achievement went worldwide. It is a win for me, but also for disabled people in sport in general. I'm not saying you have to achieve amazing things to get vindication and make your bullies eat humble pie. It isn't that (OK, maybe the tiniest bit). It's much more that you can achieve amazing things even when it feels the world is entirely against you.

What I've already achieved in touring cars, and in motorsport in general, is more than I would have *ever* imagined. I've raised the bar even higher and put even more of myself in the history books and *no one* can take that away from me. As a family, we have some amazing photos from that day. Even though my family have been supportive, over the years they have also told me that maybe I should think about stopping, giving up and doing something else and it felt just so amazing to *prove* to them that sticking at it had been worth it. Without my family, I wouldn't be who I am today, but also, I wasn't just fighting the online bullies about whether I should continue motorsport, I was fighting them too.

In this day and age, success and any kind of 'engagement' come with both positivity and negativity. Any kind of attention in the digital sphere can inevitably also generate hate. When I look at what Lewis has achieved and see how much negativity he has to deal with, it really drives the point home. Trolling and bullying are not related to your talent or your right to be in any space.

Now I have so much more positivity outside of my racing, it has made the criticism of my racing far easier to handle, and that goes for the self-criticism too. Racing is only one part of what I'm doing. Sure, other drivers might have more wins, but there are so many other ways to build a meaningful career outside of pole position. For me, making motorsport a more inclusive and diverse space, by inspiring people, both with limited mobility and other disabilities, as well as able-bodied individuals from around the world, brings a whole new purpose to 'just' racing. I know I'm not 'just' a racing driver and when my career on track is over, there will continue to be so much I have to contribute.

A REDEMPTION STORY

A couple of years ago, in celebration of the BBC's centenary, I was invited as one of the country's top 100 inspiring voices to speak in a school. I, of course, accepted the honour, but with the proviso that the school I visited would be my old secondary school. I hadn't been there since I was 16 and I felt that it would both be a blast from the past to see what it was like now through my 30-year-old eyes and give me the chance to set a couple of demons to rest. Walking back through those school gates without a wheelchair and with all of my experiences and successes on board felt like a real full-circle story.

As soon as I arrived, I saw several of the same teachers, including the head and my favourite teacher, Alec's uncle. I went into the music block and it was overwhelming: the teachers who remembered my friends and me treated me like a conquering hero home from battle. So many of them said that they had been following my career every year and how proud they were of me. I almost didn't know what to say in response, because I just remembered how I had felt when I was there, like a loser, with no idea what I would make of myself or what my future might look like. I then got up on stage and started a series of talks to the different year groups, starting with the youngest, the Year 7s. I spoke about my story and what I'm all about now and the fact that I was once in their shoes, just like them but in a wheelchair. I told them how I had felt and what I had been through, and I talked about being bullied and how I managed in my own way to stand up for myself in the end. I described how I internalized the pain, but also how I made the right friends – the so-called geeks who ended up being the coolest people in the world to me. Having the chance to pass on that wisdom felt like an incredible privilege.

I then went on a walk around the school and while it inevitably seemed smaller than it did back when I was 16, I could see why I had struggled so much physically. It was lunchtime, so all of the students were out in the playground. Group after group of kids, of all ages and, *finally*, all *ethnicities,* were asking me for pictures. 'Yo, Nic, can I have a selfie?' I couldn't *believe* how popular I was, as I was still a little anxious about my condition around kids because in my experience they always saw it as uncool. But I was the *coolest* thing in school that day. I cannot describe the pride I felt inside, as 15 years previously, I had been the *uncoolest* person in school. Now here I was, taking selfies in the same location as I had been bullied, but with the kids treating me as if I was a celebrity. Unbelievable! *No one* will understand what that moment truly meant to me.

After my speeches, some of my past teachers approached me and said that they had had no idea what I was struggling with and they wished they had been able to help at the time. It's really interesting how often other people were oblivious to the bullying that was going on and how I felt inside. I've never been a whiner or someone who makes a fuss if I don't get my own way. I've always been very quiet, sometimes to my detriment, and kept my mouth closed even when I knew something had been unjust. I've taught myself to swallow it all – if I was upset or struggling, even my mum wouldn't know. 'Just getting on with things' can cut both ways and I do think that it's important to say you shouldn't feel ashamed to admit when you're struggling. My teachers never noticed, I realized, because I was so good at putting on a brave face and getting on with the day even though inside I was super fragile and upset and vulnerable. That's no one's fault, but I do think it's a lesson to everyone that you have no idea what someone might be dealing with. If someone had asked me, I would have told the truth. I wasn't going to complain, but I'm also really straightforward and honest. But no one ever asked.

Maybe part of this lesson is to ask more questions – no matter who you are, where you work, how old you are, you can always ask people around you about themselves in an open and authentic way. All you have to say is, 'How are you really?' And let them know that you are always there to talk if there is something they might like to get off their chest and share.

After that day, I had so many pupils from school reaching out to me, telling me how much my speeches had meant to them. They were talking to me about what they were going through and how my talk had inspired them and made them feel they were not the only one struggling. I was so *shocked* and taken aback, as I couldn't believe that at such a young age, these pupils are already going through that struggle. Now, when I go around the town where my school is, there's always someone who recognizes me, they're excited to see me and want to take pictures with me. I bumped into one of the kids in the supermarket a couple of weeks later. 'All right, Nic!' he said. He was standing at the checkout with a pot of Ben & Jerry's ice cream and a ten-pound note in his hand ready to pay. I thought to myself, 'What a nice kid,' so I decided to buy his ice cream for him. He was so shocked and grateful, but to me, it was just me doing something nice, as I know that something so small to me can be a huge thing to others. That whole experience at my school really showed me how far I've come. It made me feel like I had *finally* progressed.

Regret is such a dangerous thing and I really believe in reframing struggles as lessons which have built your backbone. My time facing the bullies at school was a chapter of my life that built strength, so I'm grateful that it happened. When I went back, I didn't walk around thinking, that's where I was tipped back in my chair. Nothing like that. It just marked a period when I struggled so much on a daily basis: to walk through the halls and playground of that school all those years later felt like some kind of cosmic justice and balance.

Bullies both IRL and online will always seek to pick on your vulnerabilities and try to stop you from finding your way to your own fulfilment and finding meaning in who you are and what you do. We need to be fully aware and open about the damage and despair they can create in a vacuum of darkness and bring all of this kind of experience out into the light. I hope that by being open about how it has impacted my life and how I have personally found ways to reconcile my experiences, I might make you think about how people that you might not even know very well have held you back too. Don't allow them to take your power.

I want you to know, you deserve better. We all deserve the very best.

Takeaways

* If you are victimized when you are young it can have a huge impact on your identity formation, making you question yourself and encouraging you to be someone who you aren't inside. Coming back from that is really hard and rebuilding your confidence with their words in the back of your mind can be really hard too. But it is possible. Trying to fit in or change who you are to please anyone is never a good policy for your mental health in the long run, so as soon as you are out of a school-style environment, really make sure you seek friends whose values tally with yours. They might not be the 'cool kids', but that doesn't mean they aren't cool.
* Even if you are not the target of bullying online, we can all be affected by the tone of content we consume, whether it's comments beneath people's pictures or in articles. It is very easy to feel saddened and depressed after reading that kind of negativity, even if it wasn't directed at you in any way. It can be appalling and have a big impact on your mental state. Really make a concerted effort to step away when you are feeling down – no matter how that emotion has been generated – and make sure you only follow accounts that you find uplifting rather than those that spin more of the toxicity.
* There will undoubtedly be moments in life when you prove bullies and naysayers wrong and those moments will feel

extremely sweet. But you have to try to release your feelings about your bullies and not allow them to continue to occupy space in your mind. While they can motivate you to be the best version of yourself, don't just do things because it would impress your bully or make them see the error of their ways. Don't give them the oxygen to have any impact on your life. This is really hard to do in practice – even now, there are things that bullies have said that are stuck under my skin. But it is a worthy aim.

LESSON FOUR

FIND WHAT WORKS FOR YOU

I'm a big believer in mental self-reliance as the key to unlocking confidence, self-esteem and happiness in all areas of your life. You have no say in your physical abilities, your IQ, who your parents are or where you were born. But if you can learn to trust yourself and build an inner core of steel, it's amazing how that can translate to positivity and the achievement of your goals. Even though I often ask others for help, I know that when it comes to it I can 100 per cent rely on myself to figure out a situation. I might encounter physical barriers, but I use my mental strength to come up with solutions. Not everyone will agree with me, but I believe that in order to be a good friend, partner or family member, you have to figure out your own life first. Until you begin to take responsibility for yourself, and try to stand on your own two feet – at least metaphorically – you will struggle to effect any kind of positive change in your life.

Because of my condition, I have become a great problem-solver and I believe that looking at complications from a different angle can really help you overcome them. Let's take a physical obstacle or activity, like carrying liquid in an open cup. With the way that

I move, if I were to carry say a glass of water from the kitchen to the sofa, the water would end up swilling from one side to another until it ended up spilling all over the floor. Obviously not ideal. Because I'm very heavy footed like King Kong when I walk, whenever I land, the water jumps. After experimenting with all sorts of water levels, I found that it was actually adding *ice* that stopped the water splashing out. The more ice the better. It's a simple workaround that then enables me to live like everyone else and means I can take what I have learned about liquid in a cup and use it in different scenarios. For example, in a night club or bar, I now know that as long as there is ice in my glass, I can walk around like my mates do with my drink in my hand. With this kind of thing, it's always about thinking, how can I, Nic, do it? Because the able-bodied way isn't the only way. Obviously, these solutions all depend on your own physical realities. Whatever solution you set up, it's important to accept your own way, no matter what that looks like.

Another good example is carrying a bowl of cereal to the breakfast table. For me, walking with cornflakes submerged in milk is another disaster waiting to happen, with the milk pouring out of the bowl as I try not to spill any and not fall over or lose my balance in the process. Over time I have found that it is far easier to carry a bowl of *dry* cornflakes to my desired seating destination and then return with the carton of milk to drown them. Another solution, which can be used in different locations, such as breakfast at a hotel when I am away racing. It doesn't matter if the person taking me to my table chooses the one furthest away from the buffet, which happens more often than you might think. I can still get my bowl of cereal and the milk to the table, albeit with a couple of trips back and forth. At the end of the day, you have to make it work for you and once you have been forced to find one solution, other solutions can become second nature. I always try to remind people that able-bodied people fall over, trip and spill things too, and that having one or two difficult experiences while you're going about your daily life is natural for everyone.

Finding unconventional ways to approach problems and obstacles can unblock so many paths for you. Whether that is reinterpreting the rules, repurposing your tools and resources, or simply changing your mindset. Sometimes it's just a temporary fix that helps you in the moment: say your computer keeps crashing, so you direct a fan at it until you can get a document sent. But other times workarounds can have a fundamental impact on your success. There are so many examples of people who have profoundly impacted our culture by creating workarounds. Take Stephen Hawking. Despite having a very rare form of early-onset motor neurone disease from the age of 21 and losing the ability to write by his late twenties, he developed new visual methods, including seeing equations in terms of geometry, in order to continue to explore the mysteries of the universe. After a tracheotomy and the full loss of his voice, he communicated by raising his eyebrows, then in 1986 he received 'the Equalizer', a computer-generated speech synthesizer he controlled with his hand. When he went on to lose the use of his hands, he began to use his cheek muscles. His synthesized voice – with its American accent – is perhaps one of the most famous of all time and has helped connect millions of people to his ground-breaking ideas and discoveries about our world.

Of course, it is not just those with disabilities who overcome obstacles by thinking differently and coming up with inspired solutions. Just think of the story behind Michael Jordan and Nike. In an attempt to save Nike's fledgling and failing basketball division, an executive called Sonny Vaccaro came up with a plan to bet on Jordan's burgeoning star power with a new shoe, 'Air Jordans', the first branding collaboration of its kind. Following on from this, Jordan's mother negotiated for the young player to receive a cut of every shoe sold in the first-of-its-kind deal, transforming the business of being a sports star forever more. The boost to Nike's fortunes was unsurpassed and today it is the world's number-one sports-shoe brand. By doing things differently, both Nike and Michael Jordan broke the mould and changed the game while becoming inordinately successful in the process.

Another great sporting example is General Manager Billy Beane's workaround at the Oakland As baseball team in the early 2000s. Beset with all sorts of financial issues, the team was sinking in the league, unable to recruit quality players. There was simply no way they could compete. So Beane decided to use sabermetric sports analytics to find players who performed well in comparison to their cost to the team – that is, players who were undervalued. Sometimes this was because of their age, or their playing style. Sometimes their on-base percentages were obscured because they were more often placed in a different position on the field. With one of the smallest salary pools in the Major League, the Oakland As went on to win 20 consecutive games in 2002. A year later, the journalist Michael Lewis wrote a book based on Beane's tactics called *Moneyball: The Art of Winning an Unfair Game,* which became the inspiration for a major motion picture starring Brad Pitt. Quite the workaround. By doing things differently, you often inadvertently achieve more.

This is one of the reasons that it doesn't frustrate me to have to come up with these solutions. But also, if I'm being honest, it's perhaps easier for me to think this way because I don't know any different. I don't know what it's like to not have to worry about steps, for example. I'll be walking along the street in London, listening to my headphones, just chilling, and then I'll suddenly see some steps that I need to get up and there's no handrail and it's like, agh, *rubbish*. So, I'll be thinking, OK, what can I do? How can I get there, what can I use? I've never not had to have that thought process. I totally get the people who feel that there should be a handrail everywhere. Or a lift, or a ramp. There just *should* be, it's bloody unfair. But I can only operate with what is, not what should be, and look after myself in that context. I need the mental strength to know that in whatever situation, I will be able to 'rescue' myself.

THE WORLD WON'T HOLD YOUR HAND

It's difficult to come to terms with the fact that the world is, inherently, a selfish place. We are all raised to be nice and kind and thoughtful to each other, but as soon as we're adults or, if you're disabled, way before that, you will have learned that in many instances people just don't give the littlest *shit* about your struggles. I'm not saying that collaboration and kindness don't exist and can't potentially enrich your life and your path through it. More that you can't just *expect* anyone else to sacrifice time in their day to help you, because often they simply won't – the world owes you nothing, no matter how bad a hand you have been dealt. Because of that, you've got to figure out how to put yourself first, because often other people won't. If you're lucky, your friends and family will have your back, but the only person who really cares about how you're getting up or down those stairs is *you*. No one else is responsible for you in that moment, so you have to make it happen yourself (this can, of course, mean asking someone to help, but it's knowing that no one else is going to 'fix it' for you – you're going to have to reach out for help on your own). No one can make my legs easier for me. No one can take the pain away. No one can make it that I'm not the odd one out. Looking after number one isn't about being an arsehole and just being out for yourself. To me looking after number one is about taking as much responsibility for myself as I physically and mentally can.

I really believe that this part of my mentality has improved the quality of my life and that it has the power to do the same for you too. By focusing on your own needs and taking responsibility for them, you can revolutionize the way you live. Ask yourself these questions: how often do you put your needs first? Could you centre yourself in problems you encounter and come up with a better way of doing things tailored just to you? When did you last stop to consider new creative solutions that could tangibly improve the quality of your life? Are you relying too much on others to achieve your goals? One of the things my disability has given me is the opportunity to see obstacles from a different vantage point and that is something I try to share with everyone. It is so easy to blame others and shift the responsibility away from ourselves in times of strife, but I want to encourage everyone to look again at their hurdles and re-evaluate how they personally can take control of their existence.

When I was a child, I definitely relied on my parents for everything. I wasn't really bothered about making the effort and I just followed anything that made my life easier. I expected people and my schools to make the amendments and adjustments required for me to be there. I expected helpers and allowances. I never really felt sorry for myself, but I had what I had and I knew it was a disadvantage, so I felt it was other people's job to put me on a level playing field and make me feel accepted and normal. When you're very young of course that's OK. At that age you don't know any better and there's not much you can do as a ten-year-old. Of course you rely on your parents and teachers. 'If I could just sit there and you could push me, that would be great!' 'Oh, Miss, I can't write that, can you do it for me?' That is natural and normal.

But as time went on, my parents started drumming 'Take action and responsibility' into my skull. Endlessly! The mantra was always, *be responsible for your own responsibilities*. At the beginning that was a bit of a body shock and I remember feeling that I was being made to feel responsible for things that shouldn't have been my responsibility. It wasn't my fault that everything was so hard for me, why was I having to deal with it? Of course, I still relied on my parents, but they started to often say no to my requests for assistance. They would tell me I needed to do things on my own this time and that's really when I started to develop my systems and solutions to manage even the simplest tasks.

I also learned that coming up with these solutions is often as much about your ego and embarrassment as anything else. Everyone wants to be able to do normal things 'normally'. That might be wanting to do maths the way the teacher tells you to or organizing your diary in the way a calendar lines up your days or doing dance steps the way everyone else does. Especially when you are young, you want to be normative, to think neurotypically, to move like everyone else. You can carry shame and a sense of humiliation if you can't do things like everyone else. I certainly went through that and felt mortified when I had to do something which obviously marked me out as different. But true progress is about overcoming this awkwardness and accepting for both ourselves and others that there are lots of ways to reach the same destination and there is no hierarchy in that journey.

MY WORKAROUNDS IN ACTION

When I was younger, I was football mad. I just loved it. I had a cheap net in the back garden, but I found it really upsetting that with a regular ball I could never create any loft or height and I couldn't get the ball into the top corner of the net. So, one day I went out and bought a Coca-Cola plastic beach ball. I never thought, Oh, I can't play football – I just had to work something out. And because I developed confidence and strength with the lighter ball at home, where I could now 'bend it' into the top corner like David Beckham, when it came to playing with the other lads at school, the heavier ball didn't stop me from joining in. Sure, it was harder, and I knew I'd never be able to kick it that far, but as long as I could get the ball and pass it on, that was OK. With all sports, for me it's about coming up with 'Nic's way', which usually isn't so different from the able-bodied way – I just need a little tweak here and there.

With basketball, for example, there's no offside rule, so I just stood in one position, making sure it was somewhere I could be valuable, without having to run around all the time. I was always open to pass the ball out. I didn't need to score, but I could be a team player if someone else was in trouble. That's how I could be part of it, without having to expend so much energy. When I was younger, I used to also play a lot of tennis and I had a coach at one point, because it kept me so fit. The first step was to recognize and accept that I simply would never have the physical strength and speed to play a game of tennis like an able-bodied person. You take that on board and then move forward to make a plan. What about if I was allowed two bounces to get to the ball instead of one, would that work? You have to be OK about making tweaks and not feel embarrassed or ashamed about them. I'm at such a massive disadvantage physically, and a second bounce doesn't totally upend the game or require anyone to change the court or whatever. Playing the game is still punishing for me, mostly because I scrape my feet across the floor when I run, so the sides of my shoes get torn through to my foot and I end up with cuts on the skin. I remember my coach always telling me to stop, saying, 'Nic, your foot is bleeding *a lot!*' and I'd be like, yeah, yeah, let's finish the game. I just deal with the pain later. No matter what kind of sport I do, there is going to be pain afterwards, so I just kind of add it to the list.

It's like my race car, for example. For safety reasons, every driver has to be able to get out of their car within seven seconds. So, if the car is on fire, there can be no exceptions for a disabled person taking longer. I get in and out of mine in a very unorthodox, unconventional way. It's unique on the grid, for sure. Basically, I push myself over the height of the roof using my upper-body strength, then slide my legs in and out. Everyone else can lift their leg, put it in first and move in, but I have to do a dip to tick the box. Yes, it looks different and draws attention. Some may think it looks weird or stupid, but I think it looks *cool*. It's unique and totally different from any other driver on the grid and I like being different.

Who cares what people think anyway? As long as I can get in and out super quick, that's all that matters. That's 'Nic's way' and I use the same mentality more generally in my everyday life.

I can't remember the first day on my own after I moved out of my parents' place when I was 23. I'd become so independent at home that literally moving from one house to another wasn't a big deal. I could get things off high shelves and had made a plan to carry knives safely in the kitchen. While I rarely lost balance, importantly I had taught myself how to fall over and not damage myself. By the time I was living alone, that was just second nature. There was never a scary moment and my parents have never felt nervous about me being on my own. All of that has come from having to find the solutions and not always relying on someone else to protect me. Yes, sometimes I have to enlist help, but that's the same as hiring a handyman to do something out of your reach: it's not expecting a handyman to always be there, or to step in without you even calling them. It's having agency over everything in your life. I may have had times when I needed someone to hold my hand physically. Just the other day I fell down the stairs at home and ended up sliding down the banister, bruising my ribs, cutting and grazing the left side of my body. I could definitely have had someone holding my hand in that moment! But mentally, I don't need any hand holding, and at the end of the day, I have to figure it out.

What I will admit is that always having to operate like this, making those short (or in most cases long) cuts in both my work and my private life, can be really lonely. Being a disabled person can be *very* lonely, full stop. There aren't endless people going through what you're going through and that is isolating as an experience, no matter what you are struggling with.

THE MENTAL TOLLS AND JOYS OF DOING IT YOURSELF

Over the years, I've become very open to mental health understanding and knowing that it's OK to *not* be OK sometimes. You don't always have to be this beaming light of positivity. When you are trying to square up to any kind of adversity, you are not always going to be a beacon of joy. It's OK to accept that you don't feel great and that today is tough. That acceptance isn't going to stop you having a good day tomorrow. It's merely an admission that you don't have the strength on that day, but you will for others.

I want you to think of this when you want to give up on 'hard things'. One bad day out of seven days of the week isn't enough to sink you. One week out of 52 can't touch your determination. Even one year of your life. You can come back from so much. There have been many mornings in my life when I have woken up feeling desperately lonely and thinking, *shit*, how can I move forwards? How on earth am I going to begin to build this bridge today when I've only got three wheels on my wagon? When you rely on other people to fix things for you and for whatever reason they don't, you can go so quickly to a place of bitterness. When you have expected people to hold the door open for you, because you feel entitled to that, it can be a bitter pill to swallow when it slams in your face. I have gone through real periods of depression because of this kind of scenario. You need to have the strength to move forward when the hand is not offered. What are *you* going to do about it? I've got to a point now where I don't need anybody's charity or kindness to do anything in the day, as I know I will be able to manage it on my own. I don't need to phone a friend. *It's true*, I don't need anyone to help me physically any more, but I do still have to adapt everything in my life to make it work, which is mentally taxing. Now, I'm in a position where, if I'm at an airport, for example, and someone offers to help me up the stairs, I can thank them but say, I actually don't need that now. But I really appreciate it every time. Whereas before there was part of me that expected it and felt entitled to it and if I didn't get it, that would make me feel really angry with the world. It's been a huge shift in attitude.

Whenever you have encountered a problem and you feel like you didn't really succeed in overcoming it, what you need to hammer home is that this discomfort is like going to the gym to train your muscles. It's going to hurt at the time, it's probably going to ache like hell the next day. But what you're doing is tearing the muscle fibres so they will rebuild themselves stronger over the next days. Mentally, by pushing yourself into situations of self-reliance, you are retraining your thought patterns and shifting your mentality. This stuff doesn't happen overnight. Of course, there have been times over the years when I've been in some kind of dire situation and I've just wished my parents or a partner or a friend would scoop me up and fix it for me. But they can't and won't always be there to do that, so you might as well develop your self-reliance. There's only one person who can achieve your goals.

As a final note here, I want to say to anyone else with physical limitations who is reading this that you can only live in your lane in the very best way you can. We are never going to not be disabled and there will be limitations which we have to accept. Obviously, I have a lot more privilege than many disabled people, as I have independence in all aspects of my life. But even people like me feel lonely and isolated with their disability. It's a natural feeling and response to our situation, because it is just often a solitary spot, regardless of your limitations.

Recently in a therapy session, I was talking about how lonely and misunderstood I felt by practically everyone around me and how often, when I imagine myself, I visualize my younger self. It is always little 11-year-old Nic at school in his wheelchair who comes to mind. My therapist asked me to go into more detail and explain where 'little Nic' was or what he was doing. It took me literally two seconds to say, 'He's at school, in the playground in his wheelchair sitting under a light, like a streetlamp. It is night-time, cold and dark and no one else is around.' I really took *myself* by surprise with this visualization because it made me realize that even today, with all I have achieved, I still see myself as deeply alone. I do not think it will ever leave me. After everything, somewhere inside I will still be that young boy in his wheelchair.

It probably wasn't until my later twenties that I was able to acknowledge and accept how lonely I have been. I was definitely in denial, I think I didn't really ever go there because I was so used to being in my position and dealing with it. Let's go, boys, happy, happy! But I've also realized that just because you are lonely with an experience doesn't mean you can't build relationships, progress towards your dreams and live a full life. Lots of people have their own bespoke corners of mental lonesomeness and there are plenty of marginal experiences which can lead to social isolation. For anyone who feels this way, the truth is that really you are not quite so alone in your loneliness as you might think.

As for how self-reliance can grease the wheels of your success, I can't encourage it more. Life is really a shark-pit and you will find that aside from maybe your family, the only person who can stop you from drowning is *you*. If it's between you and them, someone else will always choose themselves. So, you have to be prepared to be let down by people you trust. You need to be aware that there will be people who make you feel incredible and that they have your back but will then pull it all away from you the minute it no longer suits their needs. Especially when it comes to the professional world – you are your only true champion. Other people might nudge open some doors, but only you can walk through them and deal with the upshot when things go wrong. Business is business and money makes the world go round.

I would always encourage anyone to use absolutely everything they've got when they're starting out in their career. Don't be embarrassed to approach people to get through the door. I have chased people so much and made myself a nuisance. I am a nightmare! But also, if you really want to work for a certain company or get a certain person or business's attention and they won't give you the time of day, you have to force your way in. If the foyer door doesn't open, go to another door. If that one is locked, go to the window. You do not stop knocking on doors. Even if security is trying to push you back, you scream and you shout, *'Give me a shot!'* Eventually someone will hear you and something will spark a conversation or opportunity. Keep knocking, battering that door down. Don't let up until you're literally getting a restraining order (this is a joke, obviously, but you get the gist).

You will fail most of the time, in pretty much every area. But it's how you weather those failures that determines whether you stay inside the door or end up back on your bum on the pavement. I've been there before, too, by the way. But you dust yourself off, get back up and treat the experience as a badge of honour. You can absolutely blow much-longed-for opportunities, even when you try hard. You can and will mess things up: it's not the end, it's all learning. Life doesn't go steadily from A to B, it's a total rollercoaster. You probably don't even know what the B, or your final destination, is yet. It's all trial and error, it's a journey full of ups and downs, oh yeah, all the cliches. One minute you're high as a kite and feeling so happy and then the next minute you're feeling as low as ever. It's the same with me, one minute I'm like, this is a nightmare, and then I'm like, *yeah*, let's go, it's amazing! It's embracing the rollercoaster ride and knowing that OK, I'm strapping in, some days are going to be horrendous. When you're prepared for that, you know it's going to go up and down and you have to be able to take accountability and look clear-eyed at the days when you're really in the shit. At the same time, you will learn that everything will pass if you just keep moving forwards. When you get to the peak, celebrate the win for sure, but also be aware that things can go backwards from there. All you can do is try to minimize the backslide and strap back in.

I didn't always have the confidence I have now. As a teenager I was really shy. I didn't have any qualifications. I was embarrassed of so many things about myself. It's taken a lot of steps to get here. Often, it's a case of necessity. If you need a job, it's not going to come to you. Are you a person who *talks* about the fact you want to get a job or a person who goes and *gets* a job? Which one do you want to be? You are the only person who can make that decision. Turning up and being vulnerable and nervous is OK. Rome wasn't built in a day and not everyone is going to arrive feeling amazingly confident from the get-go. You will meet people who understand you and accept you along the way. You'll also get those who absolutely don't get you and want to run as far as possible away from you.

But through all of those situations, you learn about yourself and about how you can carry yourself differently. Did you turn up on time? Did you make a mistake in talking about yourself? Were you shaking or sweating? Did you give off a desperado vibe? (Been there, for sure.) Ask for all the feedback and don't be offended – instead, see it as a gift. Your biggest job at the beginning of your journey is making mental notes about how you can improve yourself for *next time*. Once you've done it once, however terrible it was, you do know you can do it again without actually dying. You've got to keep going because the next time it will be easier. And easier and easier and you will get better and better at talking about yourself. And the more you can talk about yourself, the more you gain self-confidence about who you are, your story and what you have to offer.

People often feel awkward about selling themselves in this way. From my experience, overselling yourself is no bad thing – whatever you can do to get in that door is all good. Remember that other people will be doing the same, so try not to have any shame holding you back. It can be tough to sell yourself, especially if you're a Brit. Culturally, humility and modesty are so praised, but as much as they can be great character traits, they can also paralyse you. When I was younger, I didn't always back myself in front of people. Even now, it's not like I tell people all day long how *inspiring* I am. How cringey would that be? No. If anything I talk myself down a bit, because that is how I was raised. But with humility there is a time and a place. In a business meeting, you don't have to be overly humble.

Back yourself more and tell them who you are. They are there to hear your story, so feel free to lay it on thick: that is what you are all there for.

I'm in a position now where I am the best person to sell *me* and I don't need anyone else to blow my trumpet. But I have had to learn how to do that. I had to learn to write those emails, to put myself in those meetings and rooms. I had to make the mistakes, lose the attention of certain people, lose clients along the way. You have to fail in these scenarios, so you know what is right and how to do that next time. Failure is always around the corner, it doesn't matter how experienced you are. The only difference is that over time you learn how to deal with those failures better and maybe manage to avoid the worst of the repercussions.

As time goes on, it's the hurdling of those failures as you keep knocking down the doors that ends up building your self-confidence. It's through following every inkling of positivity and using them to light your path. Nic, you turned up today on time, you looked smart, you were confident and said the right things. Or, Nic, you might not have been quite right for this job, but you spoke really eloquently. Every improvement is a win and sparks more confidence for the next interview or round or whatever it might be towards your professional goals. You're never going to know how you could grow if you don't put yourself physically in the space. You don't know what you can achieve if you don't put yourself in the running. You have to insert yourself into that uncomfortable, nerve-wracking, stomach-sickening situation. It's the only way. It's like standing at the edge of a cliff and knowing that you have a rope tied and taking the leap. You just *have to* jump. The alternative is staying exactly where you are.

When people hear me speak, they often presume that I could have never had these stomach-churning moments. When you watch a confident person, you can't believe they've ever had their heart in their mouth or struggled to speak due to nerves. But we all have. It's part of the process. The vast majority of successful people started in the same chair as you, sweating buckets. Scared to pick up the phone or fire off an email. It's so normal. I had those feelings for years and years. Meeting a new person, going on stage, going to a big meeting: they all had the power to spark that heart-racing panic. It's one of those things in life that you just have to expect to be part of starting out. Accept the fear and do it anyway. I've actually now overcome most elements of that kind of feeling. When once I would walk nervously onto the stage, looking out at 1,500 people, I now barely blink. Over time you realize that people are listening to you and are engaged with what you are talking about, and that continues to spark your confidence, reminding you of your own value and the value of your words.

Every time you achieve something or get to the end of a task without passing out, you build the strength inside until you get to a point where you start to feel, you know what? Next time it will be fine. Then next time, I'll *smash* this. Yes, you still might have these butterfly feelings, but that's OK, they'll go. And then one day you'll get up on whatever your version of the stage might be (a presentation in front of your boss, a new, more challenging role, whatever scary climbing wall is ahead of you) and it's just another day in the office. People say to me all the time, why don't you get nervous? And the *only* reason is that I've done it so many times before. I've learned that if you know what you're talking about and you're confident and believe in what you're saying, there's not that much to feel nervous about. No one knows if you make a mistake or not. When you're talking to me now, are you thinking about what you're saying to me? No. You might feel a little apprehensive, but you're still saying whatever is coming in to your mind. Just like talking to a bunch of mates in the pub. Then you've done it 50 times and you've got it on lockdown. The first speech I did I really struggled for structure, purpose and focus. My execution was poor. I strained to find where I was going and it wasn't great. Not terrible, but nothing like my speeches now. But as you learn and keep progressing and moving forwards, that all becomes second nature. It's the same with job interviews or business meetings or even romantic dates. Every single one you get through, you get a little bit better and feel a little more comfortable in your skin until you can rely on yourself no matter what the situation.

THE DIFFERENCE BETWEEN GOOD BOUNDARIES AND SELFISHNESS

As I alluded to before, I do believe you need to put yourself first at times to make your way in life. I was brought up to be respectful and a team player, thoughtful and kind. But I think there have been moments along the way when I have perhaps been too selfless, too lacking in healthy boundaries, to the point that I didn't follow my heart for fear that it would rock the boat in my relationships. How might they react? How might that make them feel? So, I didn't do what I wanted, I didn't reach out for all of my goals. Now, at 32, I realize it's my life, my direction and I have to be the one at the wheel. I have to be able to choose which course I want to take and if someone wants to join me on that journey, that's great. If not, don't worry about it, I get it.

That even applies to my family. I know they want the best for me, but they don't always know what that is. They want the best for me from their own perspective, not what *I* feel and know is best for me. So, you have to learn to access this selfish drive inside. I've learned that through being selfless, I actually neglected myself and I lost touch with my inner compass. All I cared about was not upsetting or disrespecting others, and it made me lose my way dramatically. So now I've made a conscious decision to try to be more selfish – but in a respectful way. When I make a decision, I make it clear that I don't need approval. Of course, I would really appreciate support if a person in my life feels they can give it. I just can't live for other people because, in the end, that serves no one.

Pushing your own passions and desires down is another example of self-neglect. By sacrificing your inner drives, you often create resentment and bitterness, and no one likes a martyr. This can operate on both big and small scales. I have friends who are always trying to get me to go out clubbing with them. They begin by trying to persuade me, then they might start shaming me for being boring or even rude for always turning down the invite. But I'm like, actually, mate, I just want to hang out at home, sit and chill. Who said that's boring? Might be boring to you, but it's *bliss* to me! Conversely, what you're suggesting sounds awful to me, it just doesn't float my boat. You do what you've got to do and I'll do what I've got to do, end of story. I'll happily hang with mates who want to chill, but also, I'm OK on my own! Of course, there are always opportunities to compromise. If it's a friend's birthday or special occasion, I will drop in, show my face, say hi. He'll know me well enough to know I'm not into it, so won't expect me to be there until the lights go up. That's as far as it goes.

You will find there are lots of people who try to control you and bend you to where they feel you should be, what you should do and how you should act. Often, they will say it from a place of care, but it can also come from a real negative place too. Through envy or resentment another person might want to deter you away from a positive path or success. If they feel threatened or low in themselves, pulling you away from progress can make them feel better about their position and give them an imaginary sense of self-esteem through their ability to control you. At the end of the day, you can only control yourself, your own outcomes and how you treat other people. Every person deserves to be in charge of their own destiny, for better or worse.

The key here is in the creation of boundaries in terms of how other people treat you, but you can't achieve this until you have a good level of self-control to start off with. Putting yourself first is essential to this process and going through the process of really scouring your own feelings. What do you like and what do you not? What do you want? What don't you want? No, I don't like that. No, you can't treat me this way. Once you have reached a point where you feel you know what is important to you and you're ready to put some of that action into practice, it can be a huge challenge to reframe old relationships in this new context.

Merely asserting your boundaries may really offend others, as they're not used to your self-assurance. As time has gone on, though, I've learned that the best negotiating position in nearly every area of life is being able to walk away and mean it. If someone is unable to respect your boundary, you have to have the strength to close the door on the relationship. If I don't like the way you're treating me right now, and I don't like the way you're making me feel, and I've made it clear that I'm not into this, that is the end of the line. I'm not into being around you or speaking to you at this point. Being strong and clear in your response may then spark a change in them. They may realize that if they want to be around you, they need to act differently. That you don't like it when they talk about this or do that. It's about understanding what it is that you want and communicating it without beating about the bush. The boundaries have to be real and you can't go back on them. As soon as you do, the other person will notice the weakness, even if they aren't malicious. They will see that *actually* you don't keep to your word, and they will believe they can get away with behaving how they want. In the end, the relationship will remain toxic.

By the way, I'm not saying any of this is easy. It can be really hard to put boundaries in place initially because you don't want to upset people. You don't want to come across as entitled or arrogant. I so know what this feels like. In the past, I've been so scared to put boundaries in for fear of hurting someone that I've allowed people to walk all over me, I'm still working on this today. In a big way, it wasn't the other person's fault, because I let them do it. That goes for all kinds of relationships – family, business, romantic – and if you let behaviour you're uncomfortable with slide, it can dog you throughout your life. In the past, a sponsor might have treated me terribly and I would have said, 'Don't worry, that's fine. You're so much more important than me!' But when you know your true value, it changes everything. Next time you're negotiating a deal and they say, oh, we want to give you ten pounds, you can say, absolutely not, I'm worth fifty pounds, and if they disagree you need to be strong enough to walk away. That's where you show your strength and knowledge of your own value and what you believe in, because at the end of the day, you only want people in your life who see your true value.

I'm only really just internalizing that now. I've been through a lot in the last four years, and I think boundaries, self-worth, self-control and self-esteem are really the most important things we can work on in all of our relationships. If you don't have those boundaries in place, it's literally a free-for-all, where people just come in, turn you upside down and leave you hanging. If you say you're cool with that, you're forever going to be spinning in an awful cycle of not knowing where you stand, who you are and what you really want. How do you keep your mental health on an even keel if you're letting someone else upend your life and how you feel about yourself? It's taken me to my early thirties to really put boundaries in place and realize how poor my standards in terms of how I have allowed people to treat me have been.

I don't think this conversation is specific to disabled people. I think most of us struggle with boundaries, and I think it comes down to a lack of self-worth. Of course, that can correlate with dealing with a disability because the world has taught us that we have less value to society. I can see how my mobility issues and my appearance could open me up to additional feelings of negative self-worth. But it can affect anybody, even people who appear to have won the genetic lottery. I used to think that being accepting of other people's behaviour was a positive thing, that it made me a good person. But at the same time, I was neglecting myself. Tolerance can go too far, and you have to recognize that there is a right way of being tolerant – it doesn't just mean treat me however you fancy. You also have to accept that you might burn a bridge or two because you cannot keep everyone happy all the time.

You have to be prepared to let it go and take responsibility for the fallout. If you allow the door to close and you're OK about it, the relationship will either come back better than ever or it'll be gone for good, good riddance. Either way, I've learned it's a win-win.

WHY YOUR CONFIDENCE IS THE MOST PRECIOUS TOOL IN YOUR BAG

We all come up against brick walls at some point in our lives. When I lost my main sponsor back in 2022, it jeopardized my whole career. It was a shocking blow because I had put all my eggs in one basket and everything was pulled from underneath me at the last minute. That experience was a huge lesson for me about self-protection and preservation. To look out for yourself properly, you have to spread your bets. You can't put it all on black, you need to have support lined up in lots of different scenarios and different areas or else you aren't being responsible for yourself: you are allowing yourself to potentially become someone else's responsibility. There has to be a plan B, C and probably D. If you lose one piece of the pie, it's something you can replace; if you lose the whole pie, that's it, you're on your arse.

The second thing I learned was that, broadly, life can change on a heel spin. While something might feel amazing right now, it can go sour in a heartbeat. This is a really challenging concept to take on board, but once you establish it, you are in a far better position to manage any difficult situation.

Thirdly, I learned that you have to have the self-belief and strength to push through regardless. *Whatever the obstacle.* When it happened to me, after the initial shock I made the decision that I wasn't going to stand for it. I wasn't going to allow this person, or these people, to derail me right at the eleventh hour. I wasn't going to let the computer say no any more; instead, I was going to make it happen. I ended up in a position where I had to choose to invest financially in myself in order to come up with the sponsorship shortfall. That was a big deal for me, because I'm not made of money and my savings were really important to me. Equally, I knew that stopping racing at that point just wasn't an option. It would have broken the whole thing. All the work I'd put in, years and years of it, would have been wasted. So, I had to find an even deeper sense of self-belief to feel confident that the investment in myself would pay off. OK, that year might have been a financial disaster, but I was sure it would all make sense as a business decision somewhere further down the line.

It's only when you sit down and give up that everyone else wins and you lose. You only need to lose once in a position like the one I was in and it can completely destroy your self-confidence to the point where you don't want to get up again. What I always try to convey to people is that it's the self-confidence that is the precious bit. Not the job title, the money or the status. It's the self-confidence that we should all be worshipping. Life isn't about perceived success. It's about how you feel about yourself inside and what's actually going on between your ears. You are the one experiencing the world and your life, so that is literally all that matters. Success can look so different depending on the person. Lots of people worry about things that are not important at all. What's important is how you *feel* about yourself, understanding that it's OK not to feel OK at times, but knowing how hard you need to fight to keep your version of success going.

Being without self-confidence is like being in a car without fuel. You can run your tank dry and find yourself sitting there completely on empty. Even if the car is a Ferrari, even if it's worth a million quid, if it's got no petrol, it's not going to run. I'm always trying to find ways to fill myself up, to keep myself going. Sometimes I don't know how I manage to keep moving forwards because so much of my life has been one negative pushback after another. But I'm still here fighting and jumping whatever the hurdle placed in front of me. Every year, when it comes to renewing sponsorship, I'm like, how the hell have I managed to raise the money again to go racing? How did I do it? Every year I have this moment where I think, there is no way I'm going to get there. But then race time rolls round and there I am, on the grid again.

The achievement always all comes back to me when I see my car for the first time, with my name and number (Hamilton 28) in the window. This time last year, I'd lost my title sponsor and I was on my arse. I wasn't just on my arse in a career sense, I didn't know how I was going to live, pay my rent and my bills. How was I going to build anything from here? I was so stuck. But I came through it, I think because I'd already been through so many difficult times and I'd learned the mental lessons I needed to get out of them. You don't realize it at the time, but at the end of the day I knew I had to keep going until I got there. I knew how hard it would have been to start it all back up again. In British Touring Cars, once you're not on the grid, it's almost impossible to get back in. If I hadn't made it work, it might have been years until I had another shot. That's one of the things that motivated me to knock on every single door I could think of and make myself a nuisance yet again.

One of the ways I've been creative with my racing career is to change the perception of what is considered valuable in a driver. By building a profile for myself outside of racing and creating a business through speaking around the world, I have a worth to my sponsors which goes beyond where I place in a race. I am a valuable association for any team, and I offer a huge amount of return on investment. I stand for so much more than being just another driver. My parents gave me this opportunity to have a go at a very young age, then that got taken away – Dad couldn't support me financially forever – so I had to find a way to create a business for myself on my own terms.

Motorsport, like any sport, is an emotional rollercoaster ride, full of ups and downs. One minute you feel amazing, unstoppable and on top of the world. The next, you feel like a failure and almost like you are back at square one. It is nigh impossible to constantly feel untouchable and positive during or after every race and I know that it will be tough to be able to compete at every race speed-wise against able-bodied people – I'm not saying that I can't beat them, I can, but I'm talking about consistently being competitive and achieving consistent podium finishes. This is unlikely to be part of my trajectory. So, I have to use my unique qualities, including my disability, to my advantage. I have to capitalize on my vulnerabilities – not in a way that makes people feel sorry for me, but so that they feel *empowered* by me. I have been able to show that winning a race is not the only barometer of success in motorsport. I don't just mean, 'It's the taking part that counts.' I mean that you can build successful careers within sports by offering something that no one else has. People find strength in how I have dealt with my weaknesses and that can be truly inspiring. That is how I became the first disabled athlete to compete in the British Touring Car Championship and the first disabled athlete to score points in the series, creating history in the sport. I used those accolades as part of my story when I spoke on stage and the two strands of my career dovetailed into one thing. Racing on one side, speaking on another. Now I think, where else can I go? What else can I do? Who else can I help? People are starting to see the broader message that I stand for, the person that I am and how I'm trying to impact people, and the opportunities are coming to me. Nic, would you want to write a book? What about a podcast? Would you be a part of this magazine article or documentary? Would you be an ambassador for our brand? All of this has come about because I came up with a new way to solve a problem.

My dad has always said to me that to help yourself you have to help others. That has really stuck with me. My career and my creativity have all stemmed from the desire to help others and to have a positive impact on as many people as possible. Realizing that my loneliness and vulnerabilities have helped lots of others has created a career for me, which in turn has helped me get out of the hole too. I get to live my dream and race, but at the same time I get to inspire so many people while I do it. My work gives me purpose and value and that attracts other people and opportunities. People are investing in me because my message is valuable to them. I'm not naive, I know it's not just because they are kind. When I was 16 sitting at my desk thinking, shit, where do I go from here?, I could never have envisaged my day-to-day, or that I would be able to create this hub based around something that seems so simple. I had bespoke requirements because of my disability, so I've had to make a bespoke career and through that I have created something which absolutely wasn't suggested by a career counsellor. I'm writing a book (this book), speaking on stage for some of the world's biggest companies and organizations, appearing on TV, driving a race car, launching a podcast, appearing in *Vogue* magazine, representing world-renowned brands in multiple different campaigns all because I *inspire* people and *help others* in the process. This mission was recognized publicly when in November 2023 I won a prestigious Disability Sports Award, the Sports Icon Award! An amazing moment.

If someone had said, when I was 16, 'You're going to be an "inspiring character" ', I would have laughed at them. I always dreamed of racing, but in order to be a racing driver, I had to set myself apart – I needed to change the rules of the game. I had to be creative and work out what could make me valuable outside of the box. I'm not a standard racing driver, I'm a disabled racing driver competing against able-bodied people in the 'pinnacle' of British motorsport. So basically, I'm a Paralympian in the Olympics. That is a unique opportunity for a sponsor and I never fail to highlight that to them. When you carry yourself like that everywhere you go, people begin to perceive your vulnerabilities as assets and that is where you can really start rewriting the rules.

When I'm at my races, I give everybody time. If they want a picture with me, they get a picture with me. Other drivers might be brusque and standoffish, but giving people time shows how appreciative I am of their support, so then I have the biggest support mechanism around, which makes me ever more valuable. When it comes to an autograph-signing session I have the biggest queue of people waiting for me because I am always ready to talk and help people. That makes me feel like I have purpose and it all comes back around.

I know that every year there is going to be a sponsorship battle and that I am going to have to game the system. I have to come at it with something that no one else has. Everyone else is simply saying they can be quicker. I'm not the fastest and I don't produce podium finishes on track (but if or when I do, what a story it will be!). I do, however, bring the biggest amount of return on investment just by what I stand for, who I am and what I have created. Sponsors have chosen me over faster drivers. Sponsors have left drivers who are winning races to come to me because I am winning at life overall. I know that every time I go out on track, I'm a champion. Whether I'm at the front or the back I'm a winner, because I'm championing all these people, bringing them in and making the sport more accessible, diverse and inclusive. What more can a sponsor want?

No one else in my series has approached it like me, because they haven't had to. I am creative simply because that is my only option. All able-bodied drivers think very similarly. They're just an able-bodied person who wanted to race a car, they had some talent, worked really hard and raised half a million quid to do it. They get in the car and race. Whereas I had to go outside the entire system to raise the money and create a career that can work for my abilities and interests. Making that sustainable is really the next mission.

Finding a successful path on your own terms is all about solutions and lateral thinking on both micro and macro levels. I hope my story encourages anyone who doesn't have all the tools that everyone else in their industry does to try to see other ways to break through. Stop trying to compete where you can't succeed; instead, change the goalposts so you can win with what you excel in. Use your idiosyncrasies, vulnerabilities and quirks. Don't feel you have to do it the same way that every square peg has done in the past, because when you find the confidence to put your needs first, you can bend the world to your will if you commit to keep going until it's done. It's not always about being the most likeable person in the room – it's far more often about being respected while respecting others at the same time. In every relationship, at every challenge, every decision, dial everything back to what *you* want. Everything else – even if that means a decision to compromise – follows from there. After all, by living your best life, you will be the best version of yourself for every other person in it.

Takeaways

* When you are struggling to get from A to B, you have to get rid of your ego and leave your self-consciousness at the door. Sometimes it can feel embarrassing or awkward to do things differently and perhaps you feel like people are looking at you or talking about you or saying what you are doing is wrong. Let them. No one cares what you or the journey looked like when you arrive at B.
* What do you have that could be useful, valuable or desirable in your chosen industry? Think laterally and be creative. Consider your personality, skills, history, background: anything that might make you good at a certain job and nudge job applications or interviews towards your skillset, proving to a potential employer that in fact they have this massive missing gap which you could fill. And then, of course, don't take no for an answer.
* Confidence is truly your most powerful tool. Do not let it go rusty and never become complacent about it. Spend time polishing it and practise using it from time to time. If you feel your confidence waning, take notice and really

question yourself on what is going on. Everyone has crises of confidence, but you can't just swallow it: you need to face up to the root causes. Really think about what has hit your confidence and self-esteem. Is it a person or a situation? How are you talking to yourself about it? Be strict with yourself about making it a priority to address it. Your confidence is the flame that burns to make the rest of it possible, so don't ever let it go out.

LESSON FIVE

SURRENDER TO YOUR FEAR TO SET YOURSELF FREE

What scares you? Is there one thing that sets your teeth on edge or triggers a familiar heat rising involuntarily from your chest to your cheeks? Is it something 'big' or something 'small'? An anxiety or a phobia? Is it connected to a particular experience, or do you simply distrust snakes? If you're being brutally honest with yourself, how much is this fear, or even fears, having an impact on your life? I know how all-encompassing fear can be, how it can limit and lessen your happiness and stop you from even starting on the journey towards your goals. I also know how incredibly embarrassing it can be to admit to being scared of something. Especially when you're meant to be 'the man' and strong. In this lesson, I'm going to share all of my fears with you and then describe how I live with them; how I have managed to make progress while my fears continue to exist. I'm not asking you to overcome all your fears and not even bristle when you encounter them, because I don't believe you can. Fear is completely natural and there for a reason: it's our 'caveman' response to have a fight-or-flight reaction. If you weren't scared of anything, you'd probably get yourself in a lot of trouble. From my experience, the most realistic goal is to find a place for your fears in your life and know that you can still do things even if they terrify you.

A FEAR OF SPEED NEED NOT APPLY

Motorsport isn't for the faint-hearted. I didn't have any fear when I started racing, but I also had no knowledge or experience or understanding of what I was doing. In a way, being fearful means you have a level of respect for what you're about to undertake and, when it comes to dangerous things, it's probably better to be a bit scared than too gung-ho. But tell that to a teenage lad.

At the start of my career, with very little training or practice under my belt, I certainly wasn't totally in tune with my race car. When you race a car, you are looking to push it to its limits *at all times*. But in order to do that you have to prepare it, specifically the tyres. Tyre temperature is *everything*, because the hotter your tyres, the more grip they produce, meaning the more speed you can carry into the corners. The hardest thing is to produce an optimum temperature for grip on cold tyres – this is called the 'cold-tyre phase' – and to really understand this phase and how to manage it takes time and experience. When your tyres are cold, it feels like you're driving on ice and it is so easy to spin or even crash. The most challenging part of this phase is to have a fine balance between not driving so fast that you lose control and not driving so slowly that you don't create enough heat. Once there is a small amount of tyre temperature, it gets easier and easier to drive faster, and the faster you drive, the more heat you create. It took me *years* to get my head around that initial, driving-on-ice, cold-tyre phase.

Early on in my career, I was caught out a lot on cold tyres. Looking back, I remember being very fearful of the rear of the car moving around aggressively and not being able to control it: I was never able to carry enough speed to bring the tyre temperature to where it needed to be. Ultimately, I didn't have the correct warm-up technique, so that when I eventually started to push harder, I had the incorrect amount of grip and heat in the tyres. When I was starting out, there was so much I had to understand in just that phase – the tyre warm-up phase – which I simply hadn't grasped, and therefore I always had that element of fear of it.

My first ever two races, at Brands Hatch and Donington Park as a driver in the Clio Cup Series in 2011, taught me a valuable lesson about how important fear is. Race one, I'd qualified last and finished last, which was what the team had expected, but in race two I didn't qualify last and I didn't finish last either – there were maybe four or five behind me – showing a massive step forward in a short space of time. I was buoyed up by my relative success and it gave me confidence which I hadn't earned – I shook off some of the fear that I was holding on to.

The third race changed everything for me. Thruxton, just west of Andover in Hampshire, is the fastest circuit in the UK. The car is always on its limit and in a Clio Cup car you're turning into some corners at about 110mph, which is pretty quick for a 19-year-old who has barely driven, let alone raced a car at speed. I went into that race weekend with a few misconceptions about how to drive a race car – which proved to be catastrophic.

Without getting too technical, in a front-wheel-drive car, all of the power, unsurprisingly, comes from the front wheels. So, whenever the rear of the car moves, you have to accelerate to try to bring the front back around and straighten the car up again. I was always told, if in doubt, flat out. If it starts to go wrong, the technique you're taught is to plant the throttle and try to control it. What I hadn't appreciated at Thruxton was that that doesn't really work when you're flat out already. In the very first practice session of the weekend, through my lack of experience, while on tyres that were not in their optimum temperature window, the rear of my car moved and I decided to keep it pinned, hoping that I could control the slide. Instead, I ended up hitting a tyre barrier at around 100mph.

Even though I was going so fast, it felt like everything happened in slow motion – such a cliche, but that is exactly how I remember it. I can still recall the rear of the car starting to move so slowly, almost lazily, but by then it was already too late for me to salvage anything. At that moment, my mind went to predicting where the car was going to end up; looking ahead of me, I could see I was about to slam into a group of marshals, who were standing behind a tyre barrier. You can't miss them, they're in bright orange and stand out like a sore thumb – just like me when I'm walking. I remember thinking, shit, you guys better be moving because I am coming in hot! It literally felt like I was staring into the whites of their eyes, as if they were deer in my headlights. My concern wasn't for me at all, it was more like, if you guys don't move, am I going to kill you? And then, shit, I'm going to kill a marshal, how can I ever come back from that? That was what was playing through my mind over those few seconds when I was totally out of control.

I was conscious for the impact, but after that I cannot remember a thing. Looking at the footage from my onboard camera afterwards, I can see that I was knocked out by the force of the collision and was catapulted into the air with my arms flailing and flapping around. The car then flipped and landed on its side. As it hit the track, I regained consciousness, but was totally disorientated and woozy. I had no idea where I was, but I was mentally in a place of pure terror. Shattered glass was everywhere, I couldn't feel any pain at all, but it felt like this *cold place*. I was lying on my side and I could touch the tarmac with my hand. When I looked up I could see the passenger window above me, which had now become my roof. It was so bizarre – when you sit in a car, you never think you'd ever be in it in that position.

Suddenly, I saw the engine and bonnet area start to smoke and that was when the anxiety truly set in. My muddled mind just went to, is this thing going to set alight? We're all so used to watching car explosions on our TV screens and up to that point I'd never been given the reassurance that it was very unlikely that a race car would ever explode. Our cars can ignite quickly if the fuel tank is pierced, but it's very rare. At Thruxton, I was still ignorant of that reality and I just thought, if there is smoke there is fire and if there is fire it's going to explode and I'm going to burn to death. I remember taking off my steering wheel to give myself more room to get out and I threw it against the window before I realized I actually couldn't move at all. I was pinned in on my side, still strapped into my seat, and I would have had to go against gravity to get myself upright. I wasn't sure if I would be able to do that and I knew I wasn't going to be able to do it at speed. I suddenly felt like I couldn't breathe. This was it, I was stuck in a car that was going to blow.

Before that happened, a marshal, who obviously was unhurt after my collision into his tyre barrier, had arrived at the car. I was still frozen in shock and I now realize how lucky I had been. We always have an 'in-car' fire extinguisher, which is activated by the driver pushing a button; generally, the canister is heavily secured, so it does not move in high-impact situations. However, back then in the Clio Cup car, the canister was very exposed and secured into the cockpit on the passenger side. Looking again at the onboard camera, when I hit the wall and flipped, the canister came loose and flew millimetres past my head. Of all the potential harm that could have come to me in that crash, it was that canister that could have caused brain damage – I mean more than I've got already – and potentially could have killed me. After my accident, the Championship changed their protocol on where the fire extinguisher canister was stationed because it had been such a close call.

Anyway, just imagine how I was feeling in that car. The blood pumping through my eyes and ears, totally spinning with adrenaline nearly blinding me and *still* strapped into my seat. As the marshal leaned in to help pull me out, the first thing he said, chuckling to himself, was, 'Oh dear, Lewis isn't going to be impressed with *this*, is he?' The most *insensitive* comment I could ever have wished for in that moment. Physically, aside from being knocked out, I was entirely unscathed by the whole ordeal. Our cars have a roll cage, so while everything on the outside was destroyed and totally written off, the inside of the car had remained intact, so I was untouched. But that crash had a huge impact on me mentally. That was down to several factors beyond the simple fact that I'd been in a scary accident, and one of them was immediately being confronted with how much I had let everyone down. No 'Are you OK?' Just, 'Lewis (and in my head, that meant my whole family) is going to be *so* disappointed in you.' One of the downsides of being related to arguably the most successful human to have ever sat behind the steering wheel of a race car is that even at my most vulnerable moment, when I was in the midst of experiencing what to this day I class as the scariest, closest-to-death moment of my life, people will *still* compare me to him.

My next thoughts turned to my dad. He had always drummed into me that I couldn't make mistakes and I *couldn't* crash because of the financial cost of doing so. I felt sick to my stomach thinking about how disappointed in me he was going to be and, instead of subsiding, the panic rose. I felt like I'd let so many people down and had destroyed my whole weekend before it had even started. It was the first mistake I'd ever made, but it felt at the time like I'd proven everyone who had ever doubted me right. I wasn't good enough and I had embarrassed my family and the Hamilton name.

Even though it was only my third ever race, the press picked up on the story right away and the biggest motorsport magazine and website published a piece online with the headline *Lewis Hamilton's Brother Survives Deathly Crash.* My mum wasn't at the track that day, so reading that story was the first she heard of it – before she'd been able to contact me or the team. I was at the medical centre getting a full check-up and therefore out of contact, so she was beside herself, bawling her eyes out. She didn't know if I was safe or what had happened, so she was absolutely panicking. The whole thing was awful for everyone, and I felt so incredibly responsible. I was scared about the accident because I didn't really know how or why it had happened. My dad's initial reaction was anger. I think it was how he expressed his fear, but back then it just felt like a dagger to the heart – in my mind at least, I've just cheated death and my dad is furious with me. I've always been scared to embarrass my family and now I felt I'd done that on a huge, public stage.

YOUR INITIAL REACTION TO TRAUMATIC EVENTS CAN HAVE LONG-LASTING CONSEQUENCES

The team drove from Andover to Birmingham, which is about a four-hour round trip, picked up a spare car and brought it back to the track, so the next day I was expected to get straight back in for qualifying, facing the same corner. The medical team had cleared me to race, so it was my job to suck it up and get on with it. You always have a choice whether you drive or not and *technically* I could have chosen to sit it out. But I knew I couldn't. Part of that was absolutely about digging deep for the sake of my family and team. The amount of effort and time invested in picking up and preparing this spare car . . . the least I could do was drive it after the mess I'd made. It didn't matter where I finished, but I needed to show everyone, including myself, that I had the strength to push through the fear.

On the evening of the crash, Lewis had called and counselled me that I had to go through the same corner as if nothing had happened. As fast as I possibly could, at the same speed as before I'd had the crash. It was the only way I could stop it becoming a problem and impacting my mentality. Over time as a driver, you learn that when you have an accident, you absolutely have to jump back in at the very next session and go through the same corner as fast as you had done before the crash – otherwise it will always be on your mind. If you don't, you'll lift earlier, go slower through the corner and you'll constantly lose time. I've got to a point now where even if I've had an oversteer moment and I've had to manage it at high speed, I know I can control it and I'm not plagued with the memories of what happened. It's just another day in the office and it's part of being on the limit.

But back then, after what I'd experienced, I really didn't want to be in that car. I was *shit scared.* The thing that got me through was the knowledge that if I didn't push through this initial fear barrier, I might build it up into something insurmountable and it could perhaps ruin my entire career behind the wheel. I knew there would be three weeks before my next race and that if I left my mental relationship with the car where it was, with me lying pinned on my side after writing it off, I'd be sat at home catastrophizing. I needed to end the weekend back on a higher level of confidence or I might never be able to do it again. Almost like when you put on an episode of a comedy show after watching a scary film to try to avoid nightmares (or maybe that's just me . . .). I needed to change the energy, but oh my God, it was awful. While I tried to follow Lewis's advice, when I approached the corner, I lost my nerve and took it easy – which of course meant I lost a lot of time, lap after lap. I did get back in the driving seat that day and that definitely helped me continue with the season and not totally lose my nerve the following race weekend. But I wasn't able to leave my fear at the track that day.

Today I share Lewis's mentality, but I had to gain the experience I have now to be able to see through his eyes and understand that his advice was the best I could have been given. At the time, it just seemed like too much was being asked of me. It's taken me a long time to get there and a lot of therapy to support me in that journey. Full transparency, I couldn't get the images of what had happened that day out of my mind for years. It had really affected me and continued to massively affect me. I got through Thruxton that weekend, hating every minute of it – and so did my family. Even though I had tried so hard at the time to stand up to it, the track became a tarnish, a stain on my mental strength for a long time afterwards.

The next year, 2012, I had a brand-new car that I was 'running in' at Thruxton. So, I wasn't quite so nervous, I knew I didn't have to push myself or the car because we were just breaking it in. The Saturday of qualifying was a typical British washout. Absolutely miserable and, even worse, it was *freezing* cold. Lower temperatures have a particular impact on my legs, making my muscles harder to move and manipulate. On cold days, it feels like it takes more effort to pick up my legs and move them in any direction. I remember sitting in Drivers' Briefing and thinking, gosh, we're literally about to go into qualifying – like, now. It's Thruxton. I nearly killed myself here just 12 months ago and my legs feel like stone. My chest was tight and I was incredibly nervous.

But on the other hand, it was raining, and I have always felt I drive best in the wet. As soon as I got into the car, the adrenaline took over in a good way and all the worry about my previous experience and the daunting task of driving Thruxton just lifted. The moment my engine started, my focus went onto the job in hand and on that day, I can't really tell you why, outside of it being rainy, I felt completely at one with the car.

Qualifying had started and it was absolutely pouring down and I was splashing through the puddles trying to find where the grip was. In that process, the car moves around a lot, but it felt like I couldn't put a foot wrong. I was just driving the session and the conditions in front of me – no overdriving or desperately attacking, or even overthinking it. I was just relaxed. I didn't really consider or worry about the corner I had crashed at the year before. Or any of the corners. I just drove.

In motorsport there is a saying – slow in, fast out. The last corner at Thruxton is a chicane which you approach at full speed, going probably 115mph. My teammate was in front of me and I could see him braking quite early. Instead, because I felt so confident, I was braking later, but being really patient through the right, left, right; I didn't overdrive the middle of the corner. I was just floating over the curbs, then modulating the power to maximize my exit. Sometimes motorsport can almost feel like you are dancing or skating on ice, where everything just goes your way and I had one of those moments on that day. The amount of time I gained through that section gave me so much belief in myself. When I crossed the line and my team were showing my pit board and it said I was P4 – in fourth position – I remember doing a double take! I almost felt like it was a mistake me being that high up.

The more laps you do, obviously the more the tyres degrade, producing less grip, which results in a slower lap time. But you also have to take the temperature of the tyre into consideration. I knew if I could keep my tyres where they had been for that earlier lap, I could find some extra time and maybe score my first pole position – there were only two tenths of a second in it. But on that day I showed my inexperience. I came into the pit lane and sat for a minute to let the tyres cool down, trying to preserve them for another shot on my final run. It was the wrong decision, because when I eventually went back out, the tyre grip was dramatically worse and the integrity of the tyre had just gone. I couldn't get anywhere close to the pace I was at before. Of course, I was elated, to eventually qualify sixth, but it was a moment I've never forgotten because I felt that if I had kept circulating, I could have achieved something incredible.

I know we all have moments in our careers like this – the 'if only' moments. However, P6 was the highest I'd ever qualified, so I was still elated. But when I woke up the next day for the race to see that the clouds had parted, the fear and pressure washed over me. It was like all my confidence had dried up with the rain. I couldn't shake the thought that it was my inability to warm up cold, dry tyres effectively on a cold, dry track that had caused my crash the year before. I knew from experience that when the rear of the car slides and has gone past a certain point at Thruxton, it's gone, it's too late. I was most scared of the 'what if?' What if what happened to me last year happened again? All of that worry loomed over me. I drove nervously. I was just so scared that, even though I was starting from my highest starting position *ever,* it didn't give me any extra confidence. In fact it almost made it worse. I dropped like a stone and finished eighteenth.

As my career progressed, I allowed the dread related to Thruxton to build. When I left Clios and moved up to British Touring Cars, the speed at Thruxton increased by about ten seconds a lap. So instead of cornering in a Clio at 115mph, I'm now turning into the same corner in a different car at 135mph. But really, no matter what the car was, I brought the mental barrier and fear with me behind the wheel at Thruxton year after year.

SEARCHING FOR SUPPORT IN NEW PLACES

I believe life is 10 per cent physical and 90 per cent mental and that your mental state is your most important asset. It is also a muscle.

Going to the gym, you can be as physically strong as possible and focusing on your arms or abs, but if you don't work on your mind at the same time, you may never achieve your full potential. After the second year at Thruxton, I decided that I needed to get some mental support. My parents had always encouraged me to believe that I could do things on my own and that I was strong enough to help myself; that I didn't need a therapist to tell me what to do or how to do things. But I felt instinctively that I just didn't have the tools to cope with this particular challenge, so I decided to go against their views and see what I could explore myself.

Initially I found that a lot of therapists didn't get it. It felt like they were 'clock watching' most of the time and I always felt I didn't have enough time to say what I needed to say. They didn't understand motorsport and they didn't seem to be able to connect with my fear and everything else that had been going on in my head. I was sort of lost with it because I wasn't getting anywhere, so I went even further to try different things. I explored alternative therapies and even went to a spiritual lady in a yurt, who tapped me all over to try to help me release my fears. But to be honest, I had my parents' voices at the back of my head and as a result my mind was very closed off. It really was a waste of everyone's time because I was mentally shut off from it making an impact.

It took me ten years of different treatments, but eventually one of my closest friends became a psychologist trained in EMDR (Eye Movement Desensitization and Reprocessing), a technique based in trauma and traumatic experiences. Because we were so close, he knew everything about motorsport and knew me inside out, so he understood everything and we had a shared language. EMDR is the most powerful and impactful therapy I've ever had. Through the process, you have to relive the whole experience which first created the fear, and you question the thoughts you had in the moment of that trauma. Might I kill myself? Might I die? It goes so deep into your psyche. You then clear all of that – the analogy is that you remove all the rubble that's inside – and then you rewire and rebuild it for the present. How would a lap at Thruxton look to you today? How would you want to drive Thruxton, how would you want to feel at Thruxton? I spoke about how I wanted to be confident, and I wanted the car to be on its limit and to be absolutely OK with it moving around as I pushed and attacked a flying lap. To cement this, we used visualization techniques of me attacking that lap, the car moving around, being on the limit and me being totally at ease. This completely retrained my mind into seeing Thruxton as a circuit I could flourish at, rather than letting the terrors of 2011 loom over me.

For anyone interested in what to expect, an EMDR session starts with a few mindful exercises – you connect to yourself in the present and work on being at one with your thoughts, allowing them to flow in and out. How do you feel in this moment? Your therapist begins by asking questions – for me it started with taking myself back to Thruxton in 2011 and exploring how I felt about it. My therapist asked me to share my story of the day, from the moment I woke up and had my breakfast until I went to bed. You go through the whole process in granular detail and speak about how you felt at moments throughout the day. As you answer questions, the therapist asks you to tap through your feeling by using your index and middle fingers either on each shoulder or on your knees. They then ask you what specific emotions you are feeling at certain points of your experience – anxiety, worry, fear, nervousness, etc. – and you rate that feeling out of 10. If it is 10/10, they will encourage you to tap through the feeling until you get to a point that is acceptable to you, perhaps 4/10. The tapping process helps you take the intensity of the fear down in your consciousness.

After you have tapped through all of your difficult experiences, the session then flips into visualizing how you would like to experience the day – in my case, another day at Thruxton. How would you like to feel leading up to it? For me, that was buoyant, excited and confident. In the session, I visualized each step of the day and gauged how I felt. Did it make me feel fresh? Maybe only 3/10 relaxed? OK, well this time I tapped to increase those feelings. Perhaps took my 3/10 to an 8/10 feeling of excitement and relaxation. I found this stage, the visualization of my lap in the future, the most impactful part. By just imagining myself driving a lap I was proud of and tapping my way through it, I felt completely calm and back in control. I loved reliving the experience in an idealized format – if you can *dream* it, you can *be* it, after all.

I completed the session just before Thruxton 2022 and deep inside I felt that something had shifted. I arrived at the weekend feeling light, clear-headed and refreshed, there was none of that dread that I had been carrying. For so long I had been trying to push down my memories of the accident, ignore it and avoid the feelings I'd had around it. It turned out what I had needed to do was look it all directly in the face and actually deal with everything that it had brought up for me. I ended up having a really great weekend and I found a second and a half in overall pace, achieving my personal best lap time around the circuit. What was so powerful for me was the fact that, on my best lap, I had a huge oversteer moment into turn one, with the rear sliding as I slightly overstepped the limit of the tyres, pushing harder than ever before. I remained calm, controlled the slide and didn't let it faze me, which was what I had visualized during my EMDR session a few days before. I couldn't believe it: I was actually living and producing the lap I had visualized and I came across the line having exceeded my personal expectations and fears. To this day that remains my best ever qualifying lap. The most amazing thing about this therapy was that it ended up being about so much more than just my racing. I learned an awful lot about myself too.

The older generation, like my parents, don't want to be told that they're struggling with anything. They've been there, done it all, got the T-shirt. Now they're in their fifties and sixties, what can anyone tell them? Nothing is going to change for them. I totally get it. But I've personally found that being open to mental health support has been a game-changer. A *life-changer*. Every single one of us is battling our thoughts, every day. Everything that you do – from whether you're going to brush your teeth to whether things annoy you – is guided by your thoughts. It's all there, shaping your experience of every single day. Being open to mental health is something I'm so grateful about and I feel blessed to have found the strength to allow it into my life. It's what has most helped me progress as a person in a holistic sense.

I really want to say to anyone reading this that getting professional help has nothing to do with weakness, no matter what anyone (even those who love you) might say. In fact, it takes a huge amount of strength and courage to ask for help. People might think that getting professional help means you're weird. Or that only people who are bonkers or unstable, whatever pejorative you want to use, go to therapy. There is this idea that it's only *damaged* people who 'need help'. Sometimes I've been to therapists who have made me feel like that – that I'm nuts, that I'm a patient and that *I need help*. But most of the time it really hasn't been that way. A good therapist makes you feel empowered rather than desperate. There is this whole perception that you need to be strong at all times and prove to the world that you're not weak. But actually, to build your strength you have to go through these vulnerable moments, because they are the ones that fortify your foundations and create the resilience you need to keep your head held high, even through the gnarliest of obstacles.

Being open to saying I'm not perfect, or I'm nowhere near where I want to be, is an amazing step towards wherever it is you want to go. Being able to admit that you're struggling with thoughts coming into your head, thoughts that might be making your day worse and perhaps you don't know how to get out of the hole, is one of the biggest steps you can make towards success. Seeking mental health support is really only saying that you want to learn about how you can strengthen your mind and how you can improve yourself mentally, not only for your sanity but also for your enjoyment of life. That is a big thing to finally realize and it took me a long time to do it.

That's why now, whenever I do public speaking, or when I'm in my race car and I have these negative thoughts or feelings, I remember how fortunate I am that I've been able to learn how to deal with them. Understanding that negative thoughts can come in *and* that you can learn to acknowledge them, then allow them to pass, has been so transformative. If you have fearful thoughts, you don't have to try to escape them or hide from them or pretend they're not happening. Ignoring negative thoughts never works: it makes them lodge even deeper into your mind. So, you can only welcome them as you would any other kind of thought. As much as I went to my therapist and asked for help, I also realized I could learn as much about my own mind by sitting alone with my thoughts. To help me get through every day, I do a lot of self-talk, gearing myself up, reminding myself what I can achieve. I also remind myself that it's OK if I do have feelings of fear or anxiety. You're feeling shit, Nic, but that's OK. Everyone feels shit from time to time. This is just a moment that will pass. I then always tell myself that if I can overcome my condition, I can overcome pretty much anything. Welcoming and facing my negative, fearful thoughts has built my armour and strength and I now try to share this with other people.

Music has also been a huge help in overcoming my negative, sad or lonely days. Over the past four or five years I have listened to two artists, religiously, who have been *massively* important to my mental growth, XXXTentacion and Juice Wrld. Nowadays, I feel that all rappers talk about is girls, money and fame, which doesn't help my life. I don't care how many girls people have or how much they are worth. Whereas 'X' and 'Juice' talk about *real life*. Feeling lost, sad, lonely or even suicidal at times. Now, to some people, this type of music might seem depressing, but to me, it resonates with the feelings I sometimes have and makes me realize that I am not alone with my thoughts. The music that these two incredible artists have created has helped millions and millions of people across the globe, struggling through times of strife, with me included, and I couldn't be more grateful.

You can't ever entirely master your mental health: you can only manage it, because you're constantly evolving. Your mind is constantly moving, life is constantly changing and because you experience so many different things on a daily basis, it's impossible to be completely on top of every part of that. One minute you might feel amazing, the next minute awful, the next minute a bit better. It might be over the space of five minutes. Noticing how you feel at any moment will help you to continue to evolve, so that something that used to eat away at you can affect you less because you've learned to manage that emotion. Your mind can be your greatest ally and your worst enemy. We are in a constant dance with our minds and our thoughts create our reality. That is a *nightmare* for so many people; it has been a nightmare for me too. But I now know that all of these thoughts, which I once treated as fact, are actually just thoughts and sometimes random perceptions. Most of the thought processes you run through in your mind are based on feeling, not fact, and that is especially true with fear. People feel scared to fly, but the fact is that it remains the safest way to travel long distances. Today I know I have all the experience, tools and skills to deal with Thruxton or indeed any other circuit. That is a fact. If a fear comes into my mind at any corner, it is a feeling and I have learned to acknowledge it, but then move on.

We have to accept that our mind does try to keep us safe. Don't do that, it's dangerous! Our mind can be like the most overprotective mother. We should be grateful for that to some extent. But it is also true that our mind will, at times, try to pull us back from things it feels to be dangerous rather than things which are actually factually dangerous. There is a difference between scary and dangerous, and we always need to ask ourselves which one we are dealing with. To be fair, I should have been scared of Thruxton in 2011 because it was dangerous for me, but in 2022 there was no need for that fear and there hadn't been for many years. I finally feel super strong in the car again. It's not that I'm not scared any more – it's still there simmering in the background. I have just discovered the mental tools that enable me to deal with that fear. I believe there is no shame in using whatever works for you, and that strength is so often about identifying your vulnerabilities and accepting and embracing that part of yourself. It took me more than a decade to manage this one, so it may not be something you can deal with overnight. But it really is possible to get there.

Through the mental health work I did with my friend, I eventually came to the realization that with my condition and how I am as a person, my mission isn't just to win races, but that the purpose of my life is being in the service of others and I use my everyday life with my condition as a way to inspire people. Yes, motorsport is one aspect of that story, but it's just a part of it. Through overcoming my trauma, I learned so much about myself and it unlocked that purpose. It felt hugely freeing and has helped me understand why I'm here and why I was given this condition in the first place.

PRIVATE FEARS CUT THE DEEPEST

A fear like the one I've shared above is pretty understandable and I'm sure that many of you reading this will have thought that you would have felt scared in my shoes too. You might even admit that to a friend. What are far harder to confess are the emotional fears we have about ourselves, fears that we perhaps aren't enough. As a disabled person, I know that, for many people, I may never be enough because I lack basic physical abilities. But there are so many other equally pernicious messages out there that might have impacted your self-worth and created a fear that you will always be unlovable. It could be based on your race or your weight or your shape. It could be a full prism of different aspects of your background and personality. These fears can stop you from forming relationships or building friendship groups and families; they can impact your professional network and put up so many barriers to connection and intimacy that the quality of your life is bleak.

A fear of rejection, especially by women, has been a constant thought my whole adult life. As a teenage boy, like most boys, I was *obsessed* with girls. I had always got on really well with girls and made them laugh, but by the time I made it to secondary school, and I was in a wheelchair, it felt like everything changed. When the hormones hit and I started to see girls differently, I believed pretty quickly that I wasn't fanciable in any way. I felt like I didn't stand a chance and that was just so depressing. I truly internalized the idea that I wasn't lovable because I looked different and moved differently. I never thought that girls would ever find me attractive or desirable because I was culturally bred to believe that guys were supposed to be physically strong and that's all that girls were looking for. A guy who could protect them, who could fight and push back against anyone who tried to steal them away. Conversely, I couldn't even stand up. I didn't feel I had the ability to protect my girlfriend or in fact any girl who might be interested in me. Someone only needed to push me with one finger and I'd fall over. I wasn't strong, I wasn't manly. Who would want me? When I was in my wheelchair, I felt beneath everybody in both a literal and metaphoric sense. I was struggling with day-to-day life and movement.

Who outside of my parents would *ever* love me? How could a girl ever see past all of my baggage?

This all set the foundations for feeling entirely unlovable. I saw myself as literally at the bottom of the pile in the fancying stakes, but of course I still wanted to get to know girls. My only option, from my perspective, was to try to be friends with them. I decided that, as they were never going to love me, I might as well just be myself and over time I realized they would at least talk to me. Friendzone was better than nothing. The more I got out of my wheelchair, the more I was walking, the more it felt like I was a presence in the room and that girls knew who I was outside of 'the kid in the wheelchair'. It was when they were able to fully see my condition and how it affected my movement, but they carried on speaking to me, that I started to feel a little less isolated and depressed about it. In my head, there had been this idea that my condition would be so offputting to them that if they ever fully saw it, they might back away in fear or repulsion, almost like the little kids I mentioned earlier.

Obviously, my feelings here were based a lot around my disability, but you might have felt something similar because of your size, shape, background, or just an overall sense of awkwardness and a lack of self-belief or assurance. We all want people we find attractive to look at us as a person and see beyond the parts of ourselves that we don't always love about ourselves, but often we will experience the opposite. It is gutting and if you're reading this and nodding along, I want to tell you that I've been there and I feel it for you too. It absolutely *sucks*.

Over time, I became more confident around girls, without there being any romantic intent. I realized some of them found me funny and liked being around me too. They might have seen the condition, but they were still happy to have me in their life. I didn't realize it at the time, but that was step one. Of course, there were girls that I fancied, but I never let them know about it because I wouldn't have known what to say or do or how to act. So, I just continued being me and being their friend without much hope that anything would ever change. That didn't mean I didn't think of everything I felt I'd never have all the time. I can remember thinking that, as long as I lost my virginity before I died, I would be happy. I only needed to do it once and I would be happy to have had that experience. But I had a huge fear that it would never happen for me.

That all changed when I reconnected with a girl I'd known through motorsport since I was about three years old. She was older than me and gorgeous. For sure, my growing confidence and my comfort with being myself around girls probably contributed to the development of the relationship, but if I'm honest, it was her – my first girlfriend – who really led the whole thing. We were reminiscing about our younger years at a party and I was just being me with no ulterior motive. I had not seen her for years but the fact that we'd known each other for so long definitely made me feel more at ease and able to be myself. At 14, at least for me, even to be talking to a girl like her felt like a big deal. I didn't need her to hold my hand or kiss me or anything. Just for her to talk to me, to give me her time and attention, meant the world. So, I didn't expect anything. But as time went on, we became closer and closer.

If I'm honest, I was totally overwhelmed by the situation, it really did feel *bonkers*. At that time, I felt I was 100 per cent punching because I was just this kid in a wheelchair at school whom no one, especially not a girl, had ever given the time of day from a romantic standpoint. I felt undesirable, lonely and uncool in general. Then here was this *older* girl from another school – a girl other guys wanted to be with – who had instead chosen to be with me. I couldn't understand why. It didn't make sense.

Having my first kiss was a really big deal. A *huge* step. I had spent years being so worried about the intimacy side of things. When you start dating a girl for the first time, you're intrigued about everything, you want to make out and start exploring each other. I knew I'd be fine with kissing and my hands were OK and my arms were OK, so I wasn't nervous about any of that, even though I'd never done any of it before. But in terms of the actual 'doing of the deed', I had no idea whether it would be something I would *ever* be able to do and that just made me feel incredibly nervous. As a guy, you want to have all the moves and your partner to enjoy herself, but I didn't even know if my body could physically ever move that way. So, long story short, we never slept together, and we ended up breaking up when I was around 17. I think I was just too scared and didn't know how to talk to her or anyone else about my fears. When you're a teenager and you have no experience, you are so tense about the whole thing anyway. I definitely wasn't ready to be like, oh fuck it, I'll have a go and if it doesn't work out that's OK. It was easier for us to break up than for me to admit my feelings, which is just so incredibly sad in retrospect.

You might think that getting with that girl would have changed my attitude about my lovability, but it didn't solve the way I felt about myself at all. It didn't cure the feelings I had around my inadequacies. In fact, it almost made them worse. Why me? Where is my value? What does she see in me? I was too scared to ask her just in case it planted a seed in her mind, so I tussled with it internally and kept my fears to myself.

When I was younger, the idea of losing my virginity was about so much more than just sex. It was something that would make me feel normal, accepted, attractive and sexy and all these things that as a teenager I thought – I truly believed – that I would *never* feel. Back then, I really believed that the only naked girls I was *ever* going to see were on the internet. It's so alienating to feel like you won't ever have that kind of experience in your future, that for whatever reason you don't deserve the kind of love and intimacy that are baked into our DNA.

A couple of years later, I had an entirely random experience which unlocked a lot of it for me personally. I was at a motocross event, something which was unusual in itself, and in the crowd, literally stood next to me, there was a guy carrying his child on his shoulders. And he had CP. We didn't speak or even make eye contact. But just seeing him there with his kid *on his shoulders* blew my mind and turned everything I had been thinking in my mind upside down. I was like, he's got CP. He's got a kid. *He must have had sex*. From then on it was, well, if he can do it, so can I.

When I met my next girlfriend, I was 19 and I was ready. I wasn't nervous in the slightest. My newfound confidence came simply from having seen that kid on that guy's shoulders. It had proved to me that sex is possible with CP and the fact that I knew it was *possible* meant I was already halfway there. It made me feel more ready in that sense, that I was no longer nervous about the *idea* of it any more. Sure, I was still concerned about how it actually looked and how it actually worked with my condition, but I was no longer worried about it *conceptually*. In the instance, we just followed each other. When you're in a respectful relationship and you can be open and vulnerable with your partner, you are able to explore all the kinds of intimacy that are available to you within your physical limitations. Once you surrender to that, you are able to discover your own pleasure and experiment with ways of changing things up. All the fears, all the trepidation, all the anxiety just went up in a *poof* of smoke.

I can't believe, looking back, how fear of the unknown totally dominated the way I felt about myself and how much it influenced my decisions. I know that there are girls and guys out there right now in their teens who are in exactly the same position as I was. Perhaps they have been too shy to ask the questions they want answers to or so nervous about their physical limitations that they believe that dating and relationships and love and intimacy aren't for them. But I want you to know that, just because we don't see disabled people in romantic scenarios in our culture, it doesn't mean that we can't experience love and romance; not all sexual intimacy has to be about intercourse. However, I do also want to be honest and say that when this girl and I broke up, the fears around ever finding anyone who might be able to see past my condition came flooding back – even though I had faced my fear before, it didn't mean it totally disappeared.

To surrender fully to my fears, I ended up going on lots and lots of different dates. It was daunting at the beginning, but I eventually gained so much confidence because you really do get used to it the more you do it. Dating is tough, no matter who you are or where you are on your journey towards self-love. It can be bloody awful. Even just sending a message on an app can feel so stressful and there is so much that's bollocks around the whole thing. You get a message and you're like, don't click on it yet! Don't read it! Play it cool! Don't read it, dude. Don't let her see it's been read. Then you're like, shit, she's sent a message, what should I reply? Do I put a kiss? Do I not? An emoji? How do I play this? Am I coming on too strong? Or do I seem like I'm not interested?

When you *do* go out, what do you do? Do you open the car door? Do you take her to a lovely place, or if you go too expensive will that make her think you're showing off? Then again, you don't want to look too cheap. What should you wear? What do you talk about – who asks the questions? Do you have a connection? There's just *so* much. And that's the way it's been created now. Dating apps can make you feel like you've got so many more options than you really do. Yes, yes, no, no, no. You go through all of these faces, but they're not really real unless you give any of them a proper chance. If you're not being your true self or allowing them to be their true self, it's never going anywhere. If you want to message someone, message them. If you want to say you love them, say you love them. Stop playing games and trying to be cool. It never works.

I will say that there are certainly more barriers to jump over for a girl to be with me than with most other guys. She can't be superficial, and she needs depth of character to accept something different and see a person beyond their pure physicality. When I was on dating sites, I never immediately advertised my condition. My bio didn't say, 'Nic Hamilton, disabled racing driver'. Everyone does this differently and it's going to be different for everyone depending on their body and disabilities. If you decide you are going to talk about your condition before you meet someone, good for you. There is no right or wrong way to do it, you just have to go with what you feel is right. *You* be *you*. For me personally, I've always wanted people to choose *me* first and deal with the condition after. I want them to meet me and *then* decide, rather than have these preconceived ideas. Sure, there are girls who wouldn't go on a second date with me after they met me and some of that was because I'm disabled. That's fine! They're not for me.

Don't get me wrong, whenever I went on a date, I was always nervous. Knowing that there's a chance you'll have to deal with instant rejection is tough, but I guess the same could be said of anyone for so many different reasons. There are so many guys and girls in a similar position to me, who might think *shit*, if I walk towards this new person, are they going to write me off the minute they see me? Is that going to make them think, fuck, *no*, I need to get out of here, I can't do this? *I didn't realize this guy is disabled.* My approach was to always address it immediately, but in a calm, chilled and confident manner. When talking about myself for the first time, I would say, 'So, yeah, I was born with this condition and just live life to the best I can really. I walk a bit differently to others, but I am an awesome dude!', with a cheeky smirk on my face. *Bang!* Done. And then I'd just use that as a lead into sharing a little bit more about myself. But, of course, you're always worried that you will see the disappointment staring back at you.

I want to tell you that none of this should stop you trying to meet someone and, on all the dates I've been on, I've never had anyone make it obvious when I turned up that they were appalled that I was disabled. How you look, no matter who you are, isn't the only thing you have to offer. Over the years, I have loved and been loved by women in a romantic and intimate sense. I have gained the confidence to know as a *fact* that I am lovable. But the idea of being lovable still *feels* – on occasion – something out of my reach. A huge part of being lovable is, of course, being confident in yourself. Once you know you're an amazing guy or at least a good guy, there will be someone out there who will see that too. If one relationship doesn't work out, there will be another one for you.

I think that, as a man, you always feel like you're under pressure to be strong, to be kind. You want to be loving and you want your partner to feel protected and supported. You also want them to enjoy your time together, the intimacy between the two of you. As a man it feels like so much is in your court. There can be a perception that when you start dating, it's *you* who has to organize the date, *you* who has to choose a good place or a place where they feel secure. There's a lot of expectation on a guy that doesn't get spoken about. That's not to say girls have it easy either. What I mean is that the whole thing is this massive pressure cooker and if you're finding it difficult, it's because it *is* difficult.

I still struggle mentally with a lot of things around my condition when it comes to my relationships. I have limitations and no one can fix that for me. My ex girlfriend used to walk the dog and go on these runs which meant so much to her and I wished I could do that with her. When I see other couples doing things like that together, it really upsets me still. I can't physically do everything that she found fun and it was hard because I wished I could give her that. Even though she had decided that she's OK with that, I'm not OK with it. I found myself pushing through my pain barrier so we could share things because in the back of my mind I thought that if she was with an able-bodied person, it wouldn't be a problem, so I wanted to make it happen for her too. From her point of view, she wasn't bothered that I might need to sit down, or I couldn't walk here or there. That's the decision she made because she wanted to be with me. But as a guy, I felt it and I just didn't want to offer her less than any other man. That's something that I still grapple with. It plays on my mind *all* the time.

Culturally, manhood is tied up with so much that is physical. For example, I can't actually dance with a girl. When I get married, I will just about be able to slow dance with my wife and that's it. I won't be able to do proper dancing like other couples, *ever.* I won't be able to pick her up and swing her around. I won't be able to carry her over the threshold. Even though it's minor, old-skool things, you feel like all these other men would just be able to whisk your girl off their feet. The same with the idea of having a child who might come running to you and want to be picked up and chucked in the air. I won't be able to do that and that winds me up. There are so many things that as an able-bodied person you don't realize are wrapped up in men carrying or moving with women and children. So much of it is physical.

Don't get me wrong, I make up for my drawbacks with physical activities in many other ways. And I'm beyond grateful to have the mobility I do today, I literally *never* take it for granted. But I still want to be the full package for whoever I'm with. You see all these things on TV and in films and on social media about these perfect couples with this masculine, physically dominant guy who can do this and can do that. I came up with my own ways to give those experiences to my ex girlfriend! As with the 'Nic ways' I told you about earlier, I have come up with a hack to achieve that within my limitations. Whenever we were in a swimming pool, the water gives my body the support it needs to be able to lift her, so I always did it (if she was happy for me to do so), because it helped me bridge that gap.

When people say you've got to love yourself before you give yourself to others, I do think we need to be realistic about what this looks like. Yes, I believe you need to be in a strong place about yourself to have a non-co-dependent or non-toxic relationship. But to not have these chinks in your armour or these deep-seated worries and fears? That's a hell of a lot to ask and really our life's work to figure out. There are also some experiences which you might need to go through with someone else before you can overcome things. For me, to know that I was lovable, I had to be loved by someone who wasn't my mum. The feeling of being cared for by someone else can help you challenge the really negative thoughts you have about yourself. I understand there's value in inner strength, but a companion can offer you a whole new perspective on yourself too.

The key is trying to understand yourself. I personally love my own company, but only to a certain point – then I start to crave companionship. This doesn't make me weak or mean that I don't love myself. It's just who I am. Other people prefer being on their own most of the time. Great for them! Some people find companionship annoying because they don't like the way a partner might come and take over. It's about understanding who you are, what you like and what you're comfortable with. If you need strength and validation from others to make yourself feel loved and cared for, you are not alone. You go out and you find what you need.

There are people who will tell you it's a weak state of mind to need someone else to make you feel good. It's a weak foundation for your happiness. I'm not sure that's true. I think it's more about someone understanding what they need in order to achieve their own contentment. You could read for hours and hours about what people might think was right or wrong for you, but the only person who knows is *you.* At the end of the day, who cares if people think you are in the right or wrong relationship? Just because you jumped into it so quickly or because you did this or that. True, deep loneliness is, I would say, the worst place to be in life, especially if you feel you have no hope of ever connecting properly with anyone. If you feel alone constantly, you can lose your sense of purpose and your reason for being here. It's literally a killer.

I was with my ex girlfriend for multiple years. Unfortunately, the relationship came to an end. But with my new found confidence, which my past relationships gave me, I know I will find love again. I'm a great partner and I know how to love and look after someone and that actually, in contrast to what I had believed and what my thoughts and feelings had constructed as fact, I *am* lovable. But that doesn't mean rejection doesn't still play on my mind. I dread it and think about it often.

I think it's partially connected to my condition, though of course anyone can feel scared of being rejected. I just feel like my chances of being rejected in nearly every context are so much higher than the average Joe's. Not about people liking me – I don't care if they like me or not, I don't need to be validated these days based on what other people think of me and my true self. But rejection can make you feel like you're not good enough. Am I not good enough to be your friend? Am I not good enough to be your boyfriend? Am I not good enough to work for your company? Or hang out in your group?

The reason rejection is such a big thing for me personally is that it can come with no explanation and you don't understand why you've been rejected. I even get it when enquiries come in for speaking engagements. When my agent tells me someone has decided to go in another direction, I just want to know why. Is it me? Did they read something about me they didn't like? Of course, you have no idea what might be going on in the background and why other people make the decisions they make, but one of the biggest problems with rejection is that it can breed obsession. If, like me, you have this underlying feeling that you have been rejected by the world since day one, it can become almost compulsive. There can be this sense that you need to know why you've been dropped, passed over or spurned.

Of course, on the other side, I have experienced so much acceptance too. But the acceptance doesn't stop me, in my core, thinking *I just don't want to be rejected again*. Even when I'm accepted, I don't think, great! I just think, *thank God I wasn't rejected*. I don't think it will ever leave me. But just like my fears with Thruxton, I have learned that it's not about ignoring or running away from my feelings and fears around rejection, it's about managing them. I may never be able to escape from the niggling sense somewhere in the pit of my stomach that I'm a reject, but I can reason with myself and offer evidence of *facts* to counter those *feelings*. I have come a long way with these issues and even though these thoughts do occasionally plague me, I have been able to set them aside and have wonderful experiences within relationships of all kinds. I just want to tell anyone who feels like me not to lose hope.

EVERYDAY FEARS CAN STEAL JUST AS MUCH JOY

The final fear that I want to share might make you laugh. It certainly provides a lot of amusement to the people in my life, and it has given me a punchline on many occasions. Fears are often mundane rather than monumental. Everyone is scared of something unless they are a psychopath, and phobias can be irrational, super random but also super specific. When you're scared, there's an area of the brain called the amygdala – the fear centre – that gets fired up. It's a primal part of the brain and its job is to keep you alive. I am extremely jumpy as a person, something that is linked to my condition. Children with CP often have sensory processing abnormalities and that can come in the form of hypersensitivity. They might avoid physical touch or crowds, as well as loud noises, because they have heightened senses. I have a cousin, Ebony, who also has CP, though she was born able-bodied and developed her condition through a mistake made in heart surgery. Her CP affects her very differently from me – her legs are better, but her speech has been impacted. She is amazing and I love her to bits. Anyway, she also is extremely jumpy, just like me, and can't bear loud noises either. I see myself in her whenever she jumps. For me, loud noises can be absolutely terrifying. This makes me easy to scare, much to everyone's delight. But there is one thing that particularly triggers me: I am mortally scared of party balloons. *I know*. But I'm not the only one and it even has a name: globophobia.

When I was growing up around motorsport, you had all these loud engines and big bangs, revving and tyres popping. I absolutely hated it because these big-bang moments would make me jump out of my skin. It caused a rush of adrenaline, the fight-or-flight feeling of my heart beating out of my chest, that I hated. I would jump so much that I'd literally come out of my seat. To me it feels like a truly scary thing. I'm not in control of my reaction, it's not like there is any kind of rational processing. It feels entirely like a reflex.

When it comes to balloons, it's terrible, because kids play with them all the bloody time and they can just go *bang!* With zero warning. If I arrive somewhere with balloons, I will instantly feel that I want to leave. It's the same with any really aggressive noise. Like loud barks which come from nowhere. Or when I watch an action film or a horror movie. I once went on a date to the cinema with a girl, I jumped due to a loud noise and threw all of my popcorn over her. The whole box went up in the air and completely covered my date. Embarrassing or what!?

My situation around my phobias does sometimes rile me and it can feel unfair when people play on them. I wish collectively we could be kinder about people's fears and especially among lads. Just as with everything else I've been talking about, I try never to allow my fears to rule me – I don't let my fear of balloons stop me from going to parties. The tactics are the same – feel the fear, understand that it's just a feeling and do it anyway. Fear isn't real. Fear isn't fact. It is just based on your thoughts and emotions, so you have to forge ahead. It doesn't affect my life enough for me to think about it too much. You're not always going to fully get over your fears, but you can take them by the horns and accept that they are a part of your experience of life. They can co-exist beside your goals; you can have phobias and be confident. You can be scared of rejection and love yourself. You can be terrified and go full throttle into a corner. Two things can be true at the same time. We can all do hard things – we just have to believe it's possible.

Takeaways

* In the midst of scary events, when you feel acute fear, if you possibly can, steady yourself and try not to immediately run away and hide. If you do not face your fear either at that moment or at some time weeks or even years later, you will allow anxiety to breed until it potentially becomes life-impacting. Avoiding our fears stops us all from moving forwards. Every sports person will tell you – no matter what their discipline – that you have to get back on the horse that bucked you as soon as possible. If you physically can, try to make it happen on the same day. Squash the fear in the moment or, if you can't immediately master it, at least prove to yourself that you were able to mount the challenge again. I am a true believer that the longer you dwell on failure, the bigger that failure becomes in your mind. Don't get me wrong, you might still be scared the next day, but it will be easier to cope with in the long run.
* The models we have of romance are incredibly limited and prescriptive. When you live with difference, it can be hard to believe you will ever have the chance to enjoy any kind of intimacy. I can't comment specifically outside of my own body and mobility, and I don't want to belittle anyone else's struggles. But I do want you to have hope that no matter who you are, a solitary, loveless life isn't the only future. There are so many ways to bring love into your life. Especially when it comes to teenagers with disabilities, I want to say don't count yourself out before you have found the courage to experiment.

* Yes, other people's phobias can be bizarre and unlikely and there will be people who find them comical. What I really hope my story does is make you think again about any light-hearted ribbing. What might seem like such a laugh to you could destroy someone else who is experiencing a terror that you simply can't perceive. Try to be kind.

LESSON SIX

I'VE SEEN ROCK BOTTOM AND I'M NOT GOING BACK

In this chapter, I am going to tell for the first time about hitting rock bottom and what it felt like. And the story might shock some of you. I'm not sharing it to generate sympathy for myself or to make headlines; it's about something bigger than that. I want to show you how you can overcome even the most horrendous of challenges and find your way back to a place of mental strength. My first aim – because I feel that there is still so much sadness about several of the issues that this time encompassed for me – is to shine a light on my own experience with depression and addiction, adding to the voices of compassion and empathy. So many struggles are still seen as stigmas socially and that stops too many people from seeking the help they desperately need.

Secondly, I want to show how these terrible times have formed the bedrock of my success today and prove that you can go so low in life, so unspeakably low, and still come back from it. I know it may sound cliched, but I definitely went through times when I 100 per cent didn't believe there was any hope for me or any way out. But perhaps you might read this and it will lodge in your brain to remind you that there is always hope to turn things around.

Finally, I also want to take full responsibility for everything that I went through. Because my family is both famous and known to be comfortably off, at least now anyway, judgements might be made about how people I love and care for 'treated me' over this period of time. I just want to be very clear that I reject those narratives. I am my own man, I make my own mistakes, I fix my own problems. You can call this pride or stubbornness and you may not be wrong. But they are my choices and I am my own keeper. Whatever it is that I choose in life shouldn't reflect poorly on my family. I can now share these stories without any personal feelings of humiliation. To date, my only reservation about speaking openly about this time was the criticism my family might face. So right up front, I want to put that to bed. This *is* and *was* all on me.

So now that's been addressed, back to the lesson. After my first two historic seasons in 2011 and 2012, I couldn't raise the funds to continue racing. Every single season the fight for sponsorship is brutal and incredibly competitive and, of course, most sponsors want winners which, in everyone's eyes at the time, wasn't me. For those first two seasons, my dad had given me this wonderful opportunity, but I had known right from day one that his financial support wasn't indefinite and there would come a time when I would need to stand on my own feet – the two feet that I had worked so hard to walk on. My dad grafted tirelessly for years and years in order to support the family and to become more financially secure. So, it was in my nature to work equally hard and earn my right to sit in my race car without it being 'given' to me. I know pretty much everyone presumes that Lewis bankrolls me in my motorsport career, that he pays for everything and provides these endless opportunities because of his wealth and success in the sport, but it's just not true; it is also something that I would never want or accept. But no matter how strong my desire to manage my own financial logistics was, I found the experience of not being able to secure the sponsorship and funding I needed to continue racing the following season a painful comedown and one which I just didn't have the emotional capacity to deal with.

Whenever anyone asks me what the sponsorship process is like, I always ask them if they have seen the film *Oliver!*. Well, just imagine that any driver or athlete is Oliver in this analogy and he is asking time and time again, 'Please, sir, can I have some more?' The reaction from the gatekeepers of the money that can fund your career is pretty much always, *'MORE???!!!'*

I'll be honest and say I had almost literally *no idea* how sponsorship worked when I started racing, which sounds naive considering my family experience, but I was just never involved or included in any of those business experiences my dad managed. I now have a *bit more* of an idea, so let's go through what I used to do to try to get sponsorship and use the lotion brand Nivea as an example.

When I started thinking I wanted to race, and trying to get sponsorship on my own, I literally sat in my room and looked around at any products or objects that had a brand name on them. I'd light on a pot of lotion and think, right, Nivea! I use Nivea, they would be a great brand to work with. Initially, I tried to contact brands through their online customer service forms. That got me nowhere. Pointless! So then I'd research who actually *owns* Nivea. Beiersdorf. I would then Google 'Nivea Marketing Director' or 'Beiersdorf Marketing

Director', request to connect with them on LinkedIn, send them a direct message introducing myself and 99 times out of 100 would not get a response or my connection request accepted. But I would always think to myself, *keep going,* and I would just start guessing the marketing director's email address. In this example, it might be JoeBloggs@nivea.com. Then Joe.Bloggs@nivea.com. And then I'd work my butt off to create a killer presentation and send it. The majority of time I'd get a 'bounce back', where the email I'd *guessed* was wrong and didn't exist. But at some point, I might strike gold and it would go through. I'd say 97 per cent of the time I was met with radio silence, but I kept chasing and chasing until, usually, I received an email saying, 'Thanks, but no thanks.'

Sponsorship is like going with your cup in hand to people who hold the keys to your career but at the same time are *entirely* uninterested in you or anything to do with you. What you need to understand about motorsport is that each car, driver and team are basically walking, talking and rolling advertising boards. When you seek sponsorship, you are going out there, cold calling to sell space on your car or suit for someone's logo. There is no price list for the championships, each individual driver sets their own costs, though of course you do your due diligence and get a ballpark figure based on how many spectators are trackside at the races and how many watch at home on TV and then you do your best to find out how much people are valuing different locations on the car – the wing mirrors are maybe £50k for a season, so if there are ten race weekends in a year, that's both wing mirrors for £5k a weekend, or £2.5k per race per wing mirror. Or perhaps it's a position on your suit or your helmet or both. But generally you just get punched back to square one.

One of the biggest challenges for me is the fact that most of the time, sponsorship organization isn't face to face, it's all through email. I always believe that if I can get myself in front of a decision-maker in a meeting room, I will close the deal. I know I can make them understand me, my value, my purpose and why I race. And they will see what I can offer their company or brand. But most of the time it's just template email responses and knocking your head against a brick wall.

When you finally get there and you secure a sponsor, you feel *so* happy. But you also almost immediately panic. How do I keep them? How do I show my worth so they sponsor me again next season? Retention is so important. You never stop – I need to proactively propel the partnership forwards, so when I knock on their door next year, they know our relationship has proven value. I need to perform for them in some way. The whole process can be *so* stressful, but *super rewarding* in the end, for everyone.

Because of the struggles noted above, I ended up in and out of motorsport until 2018. The problem was that I didn't really know where to start, or which direction my career was going to go in. In 2013, I managed to get a bit of money together to race, but I didn't do the Clios again because I wanted to try something different. So I decided to give the European Touring Car Cup a go. I managed to scrape enough money together for four races and, even though I managed my best ever result at that time, which was P7 at Monza, my plans didn't really get off the ground, as I ran out of money and had to stop. The whole circus of races and prep halted completely, and I didn't know where I was going to go or where my life would take me. I'd just turned 21, I was still a kid really, and I felt so disorientated. Without my racing I was just lost.

This kind of crisis is totally normal for anyone who wants to race professionally. I would say that 95 per cent of drivers go through struggles with financial issues and sponsors over their careers – it's a huge part of the job. The difference for them is maybe they had a career they could fall back on, or at least the feeling that there were other options. I did work alongside my racing (I continued to consult for Slightly Mad Studios on the game that I had first worked on), but it wasn't a career as such and it also had an expiration date, so I knew I wouldn't be doing it forever. For me, psychologically and professionally, I had put all my eggs in one basket and that proved to be a real misstep.

In 2014, I didn't race at all because I couldn't raise the funds. This was a real shock to the system as I got to see what my life was like without racing. Very quickly I realized that I hated it! I felt completely worthless and without purpose, so it became really clear to me that I needed to find a way – *any way* – back on to the grid. In 2015, I decided that I was going to try to compete in the British Touring Car Championship. The thinking behind that was that, as the BTCC is the most prestigious series in British motorsport, raising funding and sponsorship would be easier because companies and brands would have more to gain. I was right to some extent, but with the budget required at the time being around five times the amount needed for the Clios, I couldn't even get enough money together to compete in half the season. As I was so desperate to forge a sustainable career in motorsport and knew if I entered the British Touring Car Championship and pulled it off I would become the first disabled driver to ever do so, I decided to invest everything I was earning into my plan, using savings to make up for any sponsorship shortfall.

That was a huge and scary decision for me, but at the time I had no other option. In the end I only managed to fund four races, though it was another one for the history books, something I was super proud of and thought I could use as leverage to secure more sponsorship in the future. The following year, I couldn't secure funding again, then in 2017 I went back and did three races in the Clios – so you can see how rootless and confused I was in terms of my strategy. I was boomeranging between plans and just hoping something would stick, while feeling hopelessly lost when it all came to nothing.

Over this period, I had been completely stung by motorsport. I felt it had raised me up, chewed me up and spat me out, taking my savings with it. Luckily, I still had my gaming job with good income and I had lived at home with my parents during my early career. It wasn't enough to fund my own racing completely, but it was a lot for a lad in his twenties.

Thanks to my involvement in motorsport, I was constantly surrounded by a huge amount of money and large numbers on a screen as a target to raise. In that context, it is very easy to lose sight of what is and what isn't successful. Because £20,000 is a drop in the ocean when it comes to racing in the British Touring Car Championship or any prestigious championship in motorsport. So it is easy to start to believe that it isn't much money at all, which, of course, in day-to-day life it *is*. What's more, my role models – my dad and my brother – were doing incredibly well. It seemed like everyone else knew where they were going in life, that they had their careers and directions all mapped out and everything was, overall, going to plan. They were all building true financial success. Whereas I was completely adrift. I now didn't have my racing, I'd lost every penny I'd invested and I hadn't cultivated any other career or way to earn revenue long term. I didn't know how to build a business or to make something of myself. It made me feel like I was so far behind the curve and in turn the whole concept of making money became a real problem for me. I began to believe that having a huge income was the only way you could live a successful life. Every single day, I was desperately striving to come up with ideas of how I could make these big sums of money, but I didn't really know how to do that and with everything I tried, there seemed to be a barrier firmly in place. I felt I didn't have any skills or talent that I could capitalize on and I felt totally stuck.

There were lots of toxic things going on in my head at once and they all made me super vulnerable from a mental health perspective. I hadn't really confronted any of the traumas of my life to that date, and I definitely wasn't solid in how I felt about my condition or who I was. It was at this point that I discovered online casinos. And I thought I had finally found the solution, that online gambling was truly going to be my next step towards financial success and that I was somehow going to cheat the system and win big. Before I knew it, I was sitting at my desk, winning and losing money noon till night. I had never even known that this world existed, but I got sucked in so deeply that almost immediately whole days of my life were disappearing.

At the beginning, I spent a lot of time trying to understand the 'systems' and coming up with strategies. It is incredibly compelling and, like all forms of gambling, is devised to make you *believe* that you will come out on top if you just keep going. By 2017, I had moved out of my family home and was pouring money on top of money into online gambling, to the stage that I stopped socializing, stopped going out. Every win sucked me in more, whereas none of the losses pushed me away. One day I made an eye-watering amount of money, literally someone's annual salary. But of course I lost it all again, because the house always wins. It was crazy and I was totally and utterly addicted to the cycle. It got to the point where I wasn't showering from day to day. I didn't pick up my clothes, my apartment was a total tip, I didn't open the curtains in the morning and just ate Pot Noodles. The only focus of my life was gambling and any sense of interest in my wellbeing had disappeared. I was so totally hooked, it completely took over my life. During that time, I preferred to be asleep rather than awake. Every morning when I felt the sun come up, I felt dread.

My hardcore gambling went from Christmas 2016 to May 2017, so just under six months. It is shocking how deep a hole you can dig for yourself in such a short space of time. I had been introduced to gambling by a friend one time when we were watching an Arsenal game. He innocently said, 'Let's put two pounds on Arsenal to score.' And I was like, what? How? So, he showed me a betting site, logged into his account and put the bet on. I never put a lot into betting, but I saw the website had all these other options and online casinos. I had never been to a casino in real life, but it came at a point when I felt so lost and I happened to have some disposable income because of my work with the game. And it was just *so* easy to draw it all into the website. I was 24, so it wasn't as if I had to ask anyone to access my money. Very quickly I was on such a high. I couldn't believe how easy it was to win so much money in such a short space of time. I always used to divide my earnings by the hour to try to compare it to other jobs and there were times when I was 'earning' thousands an hour. I cannot describe how excited I was.

But then of course it all went in the other direction. I remember the turning point very distinctly. One morning I had made a huge sum of money, but by the end of the day I had lost it all and I just couldn't let it go. I had to get it back, no matter what the cost. In the process of trying to win it back, I ended up losing more and more and more. I was so caught up in this downward spiral, just forking out more and more money. Of course, things went up and down and some days I believed I was making my way back out of the deep hole. But I never was really, because the next day I would lose it all again and then some.

Over those six months, it wasn't hard to hide it from my family, because I lived on my own and, when they saw me, I just put on a front of happiness. They never came to my apartment, so they never saw the state it was in or how I was living. It's not like they ever expected to have been invited over for dinner or anything like that, so it was easy to live a parallel life. No one knew, it was just me in my four walls pumping thousands of pounds into my computer.

In the end, I lost everything I had earned and saved to rebuild my losses from British Touring Cars back in 2015. Just *poof*, gone. That is really incredibly difficult to say out loud, because I know people will judge me in some way and we hold a lot of shame around financial self-abuse – but it is no different than any other kind of self-destructive behaviour. Aside from the loss of the money, the scenario was even worse for me because I hadn't paid tax on my earnings and the bill was about to land. In one of the most gut-wrenching moments of my life, I had to sell my precious car, a car Lewis had bought me for my twenty-fourth birthday. At the time it was probably the thing that meant the most to me outside of my friends and family. Yes, it was just a material thing, but it was an incredible gesture from my brother and so much of my identity was wrapped up in it. My God, I had cherished that car.

I am totally aware that I was lucky to have had that kind of asset to sell, because if I hadn't been able to get that money together, I'd have been in truly serious debt, which is where so many people find themselves after they go through this kind of horrendous experience with addiction. For me, perhaps the hardest part was that Lewis had bought me *that* car. Even though it was my name as the registered owner, it was *his* money that was actually *in* that car. I felt so ashamed, using this amazing gift to pay my tax bill, it felt like I had practically stolen the money from my brother and I have never forgiven myself for that. It was also such a hardcore lesson. I know I'm not the only person who has been down this road or been tempted into the world of online gambling, but I cannot convey to you how terrible I felt about myself in that moment.

The only way I got through the lowest moments during that time was by speaking on a daily basis to the Samaritans. There were countless days when I felt there was no hope and I had weeks of suicidal thoughts. I felt so ashamed, so stupid and like I had let everyone down, yet again. I was this sad man sat in the dark with absolutely nothing in his bank account or any idea of how he would ever make anything of himself. I just felt caught in one big downward spiral, with everything going wrong at once. I began to believe that I didn't have a future and all the setbacks that I had overcome in the past started to weigh heavily on me, in a way that felt incredibly suffocating, like I was a drain on everything and everyone around me. I still maintain that my experience was more focused on thoughts than on actions, but that didn't stop these thoughts from shaping my reality. It got to the point where I was literally thinking about how I could logistically kill myself. It was so horrible – so, so, so horrible.

The first step back from that dark place was to reach out to the people in my life and explain what was going on. I couldn't hide it any more and I needed help. Before I had gathered the courage to share what had happened with my family, I confided in a friend who was surprised by how bad it had got, but very supportive. He encouraged me to share it with my mum and dad.

When I finally told my parents, after the initial shock, there was no anger or recriminations. I had completely hidden every aspect of the situation from them, which is what I have always done when I felt I was letting them down. Just like when I was being bullied, I have never wanted to cause stress or worry to my family, but obviously in this instance things had got so out of hand that I had no choice. Overall, they just felt incredibly sorry for me and wished that I had told them more of what I was going through. Dad said that he understood that lots of young guys like the casino and that he had seen some of it as a younger man. I believe I got hooked not because of the casino but because of where I was in my life. I was obsessed with making money and, because I felt I couldn't do it the conventional way, I believed that gambling offered this magic solution. I was trying to cheat the system, basically. But there is no such thing as easy money.

On day one after speaking with my parents, I took two very important actions. Firstly, I gave my mum financial control over my bank account so I couldn't touch it and secondly, I blocked myself from every single gambling site I had ever used. Both were so important for me to regain control of my financial situation, as

I was still earning some money and I didn't know if I could trust myself. Breaking the addiction wasn't an overnight thing. When you're addicted to gambling you have this crazy belief that you could win it all back. I still didn't feel as if I was addicted to gambling – it was more as if I was addicted to making money, full stop. I definitely still believed that there was no other way for me to make a living. I don't have an addictive personality, I've never been addicted to drugs or alcohol. It was more that I didn't have a career, I felt that no one liked me and that I wasn't good enough. I believed that no one was ever going to give me their time. When I scanned back over the past few years, it felt like it had been *constant* rejection from every angle and corner, and the world of online gambling had appealed to me as a person who was looking for an escape. But I had to stop and take a breath.

I was very fortunate to have my mum there to help me navigate my new reality. She helped me re-establish a routine which would become the bedrock of my rehabilitation. Firstly, I made sure that I got into the shower and brushed my teeth every day. It was small, but I had got stuck in a spiral and those actions were the first step in recreating a sense of structure to my life. Next, I worked on creating a clean and tidy environment. That meant making my bed every morning, putting my boxer shorts and my trousers away in the drawer. There is nothing better than walking into a clean and tidy room and I hadn't noticed what a huge impact being in a room that was like a bombsite had on me and my mentality. Starting the day afresh with a clean kitchen and a clean eating area made a really big difference to how I felt about the hours ahead, as well as how I felt about myself. Get up, open the curtains, let the light in, open the windows, make your bed, have a shower, get dressed, fold everything. Take pride in yourself and your home and maintain a clean environment. Doing that allowed me to free my mind up a little bit more about whatever was going to be next in my day.

From there I started to spend time re-evaluating what I really wanted outside of simply earning shedloads of cash. What were my goals, what was my next target? That was a long process which again didn't happen overnight. Alongside that, I started going to the gym and flexing my physical discipline again. Because I didn't have an office to go to or any real reason to leave the apartment, it was really important for me to come up with a strategy to get out of the environment where I had been either betting or sleeping all the time. I was still living in the space where I had gambled away all of my money and it had really dark memories for me, so I had to get out and find more headspace away from that. Physically going on a long walk to clear my mind isn't as easy for me as going to the gym to swim, so that's what I did and, once I started, I ended up going more and more. Then whenever I arrived home, I would find myself in a clean environment and that loop started to help me foster a much more positive mentality.

Healthy eating became part of my new routine, too – nothing extreme, but I started to be much more mindful of how I was feeding myself. I had been eating Pot Noodles and convenience food because of the ease – eating that way had enabled me to gamble more. I just stuck the kettle on and, as long as I felt full, I didn't care. I never lost or gained weight, so probably no one could tell. But I was just eating rubbish. When you feed yourself rubbish you feel rubbish and when you feel rubbish you feed yourself more rubbish, so it's a really terrible cycle. In contrast to those dark days, I started cooking again, simple food, and stopped with all the ready meals. Mostly it was quick and easy healthy-ish food, but sometimes I took the time to do it properly too – I feed myself in the same way today.

With all of this routine and structure in place, and with a clear head, I could then sit at my computer and be like, OK, I am not ready to give up on my dream of building a successful career in racing just yet. So what was the first step? I worked on my LinkedIn profile, contacted as many people as I could and started to get the message out there that I was looking to make a comeback as soon as I possibly could. In tandem I also did more research around the ins and outs of public speaking and began to build on that network too. I had done my first public speech for a company called Bristol Myers Squibb way back in 2013 and after that I had been approached by a speaker bureau called JLA to become part of their roster of speakers. Over the next three years, I probably did another ten speeches. But during my months of rebuilding, what I realized was that I didn't have to be exclusive to one bureau: I was free to sign with others too. I began simply by emailing all these other bureaus across the country, telling them my story and my experiences, and all of them agreed to take me on until I was working with seven or eight of them, which obviously increased my opportunities exponentially.

Slowly, slowly the tide turned. The more I was getting yeses, the more confidence I was building and the more I felt like I was leaving my rock bottom behind. To this day I still get up every morning and make my bed. I hold on tight to the habits and patterns which built my comeback, because they helped me so much to overcome such a dreadful time. It sounds insignificant and anal, but creating these little rituals which made me feel I was investing in my wellbeing really did help change my behaviour and feelings. And over time, the depression lifted.

I'm not looking for congratulations here at all, and I want to acknowledge that for many people, the journey back from that lowest point is painful, slow, with steps forwards and back. But also, I don't want to belittle how much of an achievement it was for me to find my way back mentally. This period was the toughest and roughest of my life by a long way. People often say how incredible it is that I retaught myself to walk and how remarkable it is that I don't use my wheelchair at all. The struggle to rebuild myself post-gambling was far, far harder for me than getting up out of my chair. Even talking about it now is difficult because it was so immense on a daily basis. Keeping the momentum going forwards when it would have been so easy to slide back took every ounce of my spirit.

Pulling myself out of that depression was a monumental struggle, so if you are going through something similar, you need to give yourself serious credit for every little positive move you make away from your rock bottom. If you make your bed, give yourself credit. If you send a professional email, give yourself credit. I have definitely blocked out some of my memories of the time, I think because it was so traumatic, but it broke my spine, then remade it in steel. You may not believe you have it inside yourself, but you do. It just takes getting back on the rails, one tiny step at a time.

There is still a huge taboo around financial struggles in general and losing money through gambling specifically. But we need to break down the shame. It is estimated that 0.7 per cent of the UK population is addicted to gambling, which is about 470,000 people,[1] while 3.8 per cent[2] are gambling at high-risk levels. In addition, 3.6 million people[3] are affected negatively by *other people's* gambling. It is sadly an incredibly common experience to get caught up in and more than half of those who really need help don't have access to any kind of programme or treatment. As a country, we need a wake-up call.

Interestingly I have learned that professional sportspeople are twice to three times more likely to develop a gambling problem than the rest of the general public. A lot of that is down to the sports lifestyle, where you are competing at the highest level, then sent home for weeks for down time; you often also have more disposable income at a very young age. But in addition it's because the need to win is so ingrained and that can create the ideal environment for addictive behaviours to grow. Amongst professional athletes, 56% have gambled in the past year and 8.2% are problem gamblers.[4] Nuances like this need to be highlighted and athletes need to be aware of the risks and their increased vulnerability. Be in no doubt, this is an addiction that can kill people. I know because I was there.

If you ever find yourself somewhere like this, I want you to know that there is help available and that whatever it is your thoughts are telling you, it doesn't have to be final. Your world can spin back around and one day you might look back and be shocked at how you felt. I certainly am in that position now. I have gone up and down since and had all sorts of emotional challenges, but I've never been back *there*.

TIME TO TURN THE STORY UPSIDE DOWN

During this moment, I also had to be totally honest with myself about the reality of racing again. If I was going to make it happen, I needed to reframe the way I evaluated success on that journey – it couldn't be all or nothing any more. Before, I had only seen the negatives to all my predicaments. I didn't think, wow, I managed to raise *some* money, or even that being in these meetings and in the running for sponsorship was an achievement in itself. I didn't appreciate how being physically fit and able to drive at all was an achievement. Or even that competing within tenths of a second of able-bodied people was an achievement. Today, I don't take a single one of these achievements for granted, but I needed to have my experiences of rock bottom to help me see everything I had achieved in its true light. It is so easy to create a reality out of a negative view of life, to build a perspective from a half-full glass. Shifting your mentality means shifting your thoughts and when you do that your world view can just be turned upside down. Gratitude really isn't snake oil: it can change the way you dream and the way you live your life.

From 2017 until now, I have still made a stupid number of mistakes. You can't just build a new life straight away; things go up and down, of course. In 2018, I tried to start a business that didn't work and I lost money again, and it's not like the world of motorsport had been waiting patiently by the phone for me. I'm going through all of this so thoroughly because I want people to know how much *failure* has been part of my *success*. It's not just something I say because it sounds good in a speech – there have been so many legitimate catastrophes and let-downs along the way. I've had knockbacks and setbacks and just because I feel more positive now doesn't mean the hurdles on my path dissolved. It has been *a journey*. I would say really that the whole period from starting to lose my money to getting myself back to myself spanned eight years. Only now have I built back my foundations to a point where I am starting to feel really and truly solid, but I am not completely there yet. With every step you take forwards, you can be knocked back five. And you've got to scoop yourself back up and go again. And again, and again. Going through horrible times isn't something which is specific to being disabled and having these kinds of life-altering challenges can affect anyone, no matter what their situation. This paradigm is a universal life experience, don't ever let anyone tell you different.

In 2018 I went back to Clios, but with a new energy and outlook I managed to complete a full season. My first full season since 2012. This was absolutely supported by the experience I was gaining on the stage through public speaking and piecing the full story together around what I had been through in my life, what I stood for and how my values, which were built through the rollercoaster of my personal history, could align with brands and businesses that might want to hire or sponsor me. Hitting rock bottom had changed me and had allowed me to release a lot of the shame and stress I had been carrying my whole life. As crazy as it sounds, getting so low helped me come to a point of self-acceptance where I could share more of myself with other people. I was a better speaker because I was becoming a better human, full of empathy and compassion for both myself and others. The more experienced I became on stage, the more confidence I gained, the more engagements I booked, the more I earned. The spiral was set upwards. Then making a name for myself in a completely different industry, one which I had never had any aspirations of conquering but turned out to love and feel incredibly empowered by, completely shifted the dial in every aspect of my life.

When young people tell me that they have everything mapped out and they know exactly how their career is going to go, I always advise them to keep an open mind. You might literally have never heard of the thing that is going to be the bread and butter of your professional life, the thing you are maybe most naturally skilled or talented at, the niche that you will end up becoming an expert in. Always keep the door open, because you just never know. My passion for motorsport hasn't been dented in any way. I still live for my racing. But having this ace up my sleeve hasn't just made me feel more secure in the sense that not all my eggs are in one basket, it has also made me a more confident person and that has made me a better driver too.

In that 2018 season, I did so well with finding the sponsorship I needed to complete the season that I actually even made a little bit of money on top, which obviously helps. Looking back, I think having the spectre of my rock bottom *right there* had a massive impact on how successful I was at persuading sponsors to work with me. Every day I had it directly in my field of view, reminding me what could happen if I took the easy route, or if I gave up. At the time, it did feel like I was locked into a bit of a hamster wheel, trying desperately to sort things out and escape. In some ways, I guess I still haven't got off that wheel, because every day I feel the reminder of what could happen if I took my foot off the gas. I've been there in a dark room with the blinds closed sitting in dirty clothes, not having showered for days. I remember throwing my keyboard across the room, crying and going through the most horrendous experiences all alone. It wasn't even ever really about the money or the gambling, they were all just symptoms of feeling so incredibly lost. But I think that time will always end up being one of the biggest motivators of my life and that's why I say my most hideous low is also part of my most magnificent high. If I hadn't fallen so deep, I can't say that I would have ever had the energy to fly again.

In racing, when you can't raise the money, people forget about you and write you off. When you're constantly knocking on doors and having them shut in your face, it's almost impossible to turn that energy around. No, no, no, no thanks, no thanks, no thanks. Or, worse for me, 'Why don't you just go and ask Lewis?' or 'Why don't you ask your dad?' It all takes its toll. The power that the marketing directors, whom I have to persuade of my value and worth, hold over my life is still *massive*. It has felt, at times, like they were the only people between me and returning to my rock bottom. But ultimately, they are just people sitting in front of an Excel spreadsheet making decisions based on metrics. Most, though not all, struggle to have creativity and think about the bigger picture. They are focused entirely on the bottom line and will choose who they believe can make the most money for their company. They have a job to do, just like it's my job to build the distance between where I am today and the place I never want to go back to.

In order to sidestep some of that, I changed the way I approached the businesses that I was looking to to sponsor me. Because of my public speaking, I learned that I really was the best person to sell myself. I began investing my time in cultivating relationships with the CEOs of targeted businesses and, instead of going through the usual route, I started aiming for the top – something I would never have had the confidence to do before. I would turn up to meetings alone, just me and my laptop. They would always expect me to have a team of people around me, an agency or this or that, but all I needed was my story, my newly built self-confidence and some designs of my race car. All I needed to do was to connect with them, tell them about who I was and what I stood for and the spaces I had available to sell. I went up and down the country doing that, until

I got to the point where I had enough money to get back into the BTCC – which, as I mentioned earlier, costs approximately five times the amount of a season of racing in Clios.

The penny also dropped while I was up on stage. My talks lasted 40 minutes, but only five minutes of my content was about racing. That made me realize that being a driver wasn't as important to my identity as I had thought it was; it was only a fraction of what made me *me*. All of our jobs are a far smaller part of what makes us than we might think – we are all *so* much more than what we do. Far more fundamental to my sense of self were the connections I was able to make with others through my experiences of picking myself up and weathering the challenges that had been sent my way. By taking the pressure off the racing, this desperate need to be doing it in order to feel like I was doing something of value with my life, seemed to unblock everything. Changing the focus of everything towards how I could help other people has made the rest of it flow.

As the public speaking and racing continued to gather pace, I also started to build out my appeal as a brand ambassador and that has opened all kinds of doors for work with businesses far beyond racing. And as my racing moved back into touring cars and the speaking just built and built, I finally got myself back onto an even financial footing. In 2020, things started to go really well and I managed to score my first points in the Championship, being the first disabled athlete ever to do so, which was another thing I could speak about when I was pitching for sponsorship and on stage in my keynotes. I finally signed with a management agency in addition to my speaking agency and they built a PR and brand campaign strategy for me. Since then, we've worked on some fantastic collaborations with some of the world's biggest brands, most often focused on diversity and inclusivity. It all now folds into each other, every aspect of my career feeding the other. I absolutely love it, all of it, and I cannot believe where my professional life is now, considering where I was just a few years ago.

It is possible to get through moments in life when you feel you have nothing to live for and come out a whole lot stronger on the other side. However hopeless things might seem at the time, that time can pass. It is truly humbling to have to ask for help, even though that is literally what your friends and family are there for. My family didn't have any suspicions that I was going through this difficult time. I had kept it from them completely and that's something I've done my whole life. There are things that my family will read in this book that they won't know have happened to me: I have always hidden the bad stuff because I didn't want to cause them any anxiety. In many ways, I would say I'm not a role model on this point, because I do not always practise what I preach. I have never wanted my mum or anyone to go through any negative feelings because of me or on my behalf, and I do think an element of that is down to my condition. I have never wanted my family to worry about more than they already have had to worry.

If I were going really deep, I do feel like I've been a huge burden, the biggest pain in the arse to my parents that anyone could ever imagine, because they gave birth to this child who completely turned their lives upside down. I know they don't feel this way, but I guess it isn't really about how *they* feel – it's about how *I* feel. My mum, who is the most incredible human, had to pick me up and carry me around for years. She has back problems now, but she has never once complained. I am forever grateful for her efforts.

Of course, there was nothing I could do about it, but I do feel like my mum has done so much for me that I will never be able to repay her for. I know she's not expecting to be repaid. But I feel the debt. I'm like, *fuck*, what a struggle that must have been for them physically and mentally and what a huge pressure having me must have put on their relationship. Even though it's no one's fault, I don't want them to have to worry about anything, not even 1 per cent more than they have already had to.

As I've said, when I was young, we had no money and my whole family lived in a one-bedroom flat. Dinners were pasta with chicken soup because that was all we could afford. My dad was grafting to give us a better home. The last thing I wanted was my family to know that I was struggling. My mum already had so much on her plate. Lewis and me, finances at home and stresses with my dad – when times are hard, of course it stresses people out. Having kids full stop is stressful, even if you have all the money in the world. And I guess that mentality stayed with me as I matured and had other struggles. I just never went to them.

Aside from these feelings stemming from my condition, I do also believe that everyone has their own shit to deal with and I am very wary of advising anyone to simply offload their troubles onto someone else. Yes, I truly feel we should all learn to talk to the people we love and who love us back. We should learn to talk to whoever we want to talk to, however hard it might feel. But having said that, just because you are going through a tough time doesn't mean you can simply dump everything on other people. That's just not fair. When you're in a bad place you can lose sight of everything but your own struggle and you inadvertently end up dragging everyone else around you down. I never wanted to be the person calling my friends and family at 3am or making every little thing about me and my troubles. It is so natural to reach out to others for help and of course in all sorts of situations it's completely appropriate. But no one else is going to be able to lift you back up alone. The only true way out, the way out for good, is to find it for *yourself*. That's when you go to a doctor, a therapist or find an online community who can help provide a non-judgemental space for you to explore your problems. It's not healthy to totally dominate another person's existence with your issues.

I also want to say that there are lots of people like me who have put themselves in terrible positions through their own poor choices. *I* was the person who became addicted to gambling, no one else. No one forced me down that path at gunpoint, there wasn't some great tragedy that was out of my hands that precipitated it all, outside of being totally lost in life. Therefore, it was my responsibility to change things. A lot of the damage I've dealt with in my life has been self-inflicted.

Sharing my feelings and struggles with the people I'm close to is something I am still working on today. I know that I have my mum there to talk to if I need to and she would *always* want to hear from me. But the last thing I want is for her to be lying in bed at night thinking about my issues. When it came to my gambling, I only called her when it was too late – when I had run out of money and realized I had a real problem. I didn't want my family to bail me out financially or mentally, but I had to swallow that, eat humble pie and share my struggles and poor choices before I could pull myself back and go out to fix everything.

If I were to give someone else advice, I'd 100 per cent say lean on your loved ones – just not indefinitely. Opening up your internal life to the people who care about you can actually end up *saving* your life, but when it comes to getting your life back on track, it is something *you* have to seek deep inside.

I am happy in retrospect that I did keep the grief my gambling caused my family to a minimum. Even though mentally it has been harder to get through everything, because I haven't leaned much on other people, I now do feel less guilty and more content. That is something I have to grapple with myself, for sure, and I haven't always drawn that line in the right place.

My rock bottom is still with me today: it is part of who I am and always will be. It has shaped my motivations, drives and decisions. Often when people have hard times, they want to shroud them and hide them and turn them into skeletons in the closet. I truly believe that is a terrible way of dealing with them. You have to be *naked* about it. It's there, it's in the room, you can't make it disappear. All you can do is to find a comfortable way for it to be in your life, no longer defining it, but certainly still a part of who you are. Do I ever want to go back there? Absolutely not. In order to avoid that, I'm going to take all the steps I possibly can. But I can't erase it, it's a scar on my life, like any of the scars I bear on my skin.

Sweeping things like this under the rug is the most detrimental thing you can do because owning up to your mistakes and taking responsibility for them are the only ways you can move forwards without them holding you back. Yep, that was a mistake, that was a dark time. But I'm proud of my mistakes, I'm proud of my dark times. I talk about them on stage – I don't go into this depth – but I say on stage that there were times in my life where I preferred to be asleep rather than awake. Because that was true. When I went to bed after losing all that money, I just felt like no one could get to me, like it was the only time I was safe. Then when I woke up in the morning, it was like, shit, it's another day in this *hell* that I've made for myself. Where do I go, what do I do? But I'm so proud to be able to talk about it because it shows that I did survive it. I'm out the other side, even though I thought I was going to drown. And because of everything that time has propelled me to achieve since, that dark moment has almost become a best friend, a companion in my life.

There are very few mistakes you can't come back from, though of course there are also worse addictions than gambling. It could have been booze or drugs, either of which could have wreaked a terrible impact on my physical as well as my mental health. I could have been sitting here with one kidney or struggling with breathing problems. In terms of my physical health, I'm great now and I feel extremely fortunate for that. I'm constantly thinking about how I can continue building and moving forwards and hopefully get further and further away from that rock-bottom position.

I still feel like people judge your success by how much money you have. I absolutely don't believe in those standards or framework any more and I feel very grateful to be free from that. In this moment, I do feel I'm successful. If you look at my story, you can't not see that. But I don't have some huge house or millions of pounds. I'm not dripping in diamonds or flying around in private jets. None of these things matter. I've come from being a boy who felt low in himself and was constantly told by his peers that he would never amount to anything. I was a dweeb, a nerd, uncool; I was ugly. It was pointless me even being there. Whereas today I am a strong character who has achieved history in motorsport and I continue to be a strong character who inspires those around me.

But you don't need to have these big trophies or certificates or credentials to be successful. Success is what you *deem it* and for me so much of that is about the journey. Me punching the air after achieving my career-best result of P6 in a BTCC race might mean nothing to someone else, but to me, it's *everything*. To a young disabled person, walking up and down steps unaided could mean everything – that's their success. To somebody else it might seem like nothing. It's all relative and unique and totally about your personal perspective. For me to have driven my best ever qualifying lap, with my car on the limit at Thruxton, was a massive mental achievement to me. To have been able to break through that mental barrier and prove to myself that I could overcome it was a huge milestone of success. Overcoming my fears of rejection and intimacy have also been huge success stories for me.

The feeling of achievement is like a drug in itself and I do think it is possible to become addicted to moments of success. The idea that I could feel successful in motorsport and accepted by everyone was intoxicating, especially after years of constant rejection and people saying that I was just not good enough. I definitely want to feel that again and that makes you build up the pressure on yourself to get back there. Motorsport is 95 per cent disappointment, but you live for the 5 per cent. Most of the time it's rubbish. But as I've always said, a bad day in a touring car is better than a day *without* being in a touring car at all. Even though I might be disappointed, I still want it more than anything else in the world. I'd rather be disappointed at Brands Hatch than disappointed sitting doing a job that I didn't love.

We should all expect many failures along our roads and know that they are part of what is to come – in ways that we will probably never understand until we can sit back and look at the bigger picture over a number of years. With the power of hindsight, I can see that I'm out of the hole that I was in and that is an amazing achievement, something I feel incredibly proud of. But I can also see that that awful time was an amazing period in my life, because it has shaped me so profoundly. I'm so glad I went through that, because I wouldn't be sitting here writing this book if I hadn't. I've earned back the life savings that I lost and I'm building a career in different directions, creating something more and more positive, which is full of personal joy every day, and that is all because I reached my rock bottom. This has all been a product of my mindset, literally those few inches between my ears, and proof, I hope to everyone, of the incredible value that mental health and mental strength can bring to your life, your fulfilment and your happiness.

I feel so excited about where I'm going, what I've been doing and where I plan to be. I am driving it constantly and I'm now making the right decisions at the right time. I have teams of people, all great people, working with me to amplify that drive and impact. You have to give parts of yourself to make good things happen, and to help yourself you have to help others too. I'm focused on helping more people and that has created many more opportunities than I would have created on my own. It feels strange to say but, believe it or not, I really am grateful to have had such a dreadful time.

Takeaways

* There are so many varied ways that addiction can creep into your life and a lot of them don't actually look like a soap opera or how you might imagine them to. I was able to sink so deeply into my hole, to hit rock bottom, with

literally not one other soul being any the wiser. If you ever find yourself in a similar position to me, free help is available out there. You can call GamCare 24/7 and speak immediately to an advisor – they also have messaging-service options, as well as a chatroom. If you ever struggle with suicidal thoughts, the Samaritans are always there for you. Their details and further resources can be found at the back of this book.

* Turning your life around from this kind of horror show is hard, but it can be done, so never lose hope. The first step for me was to confide in someone I trusted and then it was just a case of baby steps back to my old self, my old life, but with a new outlook. I would really suggest you do the same. One of the biggest parts of that process was changing my mindset and re-evaluating all the things that I had seen as such abject failures. The things that had led me down the path to financial ruin. By reframing a lot of those beliefs about myself, I was able to start again without all the negative emotion that I had been carrying.
* Wear your failures like badges of honour. Those awful times were horrendous to live through, but they also *made* me. Finding gratitude even in the worst weeks and months of my life has made me feel like there is literally nothing that could ever properly pull me down and there is such a sense of liberation and strength in that.

LESSON SEVEN

TRY TILL YOU DIE – PERSEVERANCE IS A TRUE SUPERPOWER

My final lesson is the one that has probably served me the best in life. It's also one which is most often forgotten in the noise of the 'instant success stories' we so often see on social media highlight reels. We live in an age where fame, fortune and apparent happiness seem to be available at the click of a button, with teenagers living in extravagant palaces and flying on private jets paid for by income created via their phones. This kind of success seems divorced from any real effort and very different from, say, the success of an athlete who might have sacrificed most of his or her young life to better themselves at a sport. We can see how much goes into that more traditional kind of success. With today's overnight viral sensations, the relationship between graft and outcome seems to have totally broken down. But of course, this kind of success is only available to a tiny proportion of TikTok stars, and it belies the reality that, for most of us, achievement and riches aren't ever going to just fall into our laps.

When I talk about perseverance, I don't just mean getting back up when you're knocked down once. Or twice. I'm talking about throwing yourself back in the ring when you have failed 50 times. Or 100 times. It's the diametric opposite of everything that we see on our screens. Of all the topics I'm booked to speak about, it's overcoming obstacles in the face of adversity that gets the most requests. For me, the number-one tool in the kit for that journey is *perseverance* and the reason I always emphasize its value here is that you *are* going to get knocked back along the road – that is an *inevitability*. As you work through the steps towards your goals, you are going to find yourself on your arse and there will be times that are emotionally and materially tough. You cannot set out to reach any kind of target with ego and pride in the driving seat, because the falls are literally inbuilt into the journey. There will be twists and turns and spokes in the road, snakes and mistakes which take you right back down to zero. The only thing that is going to stand between you and the finish line you dream of is your inner resolve to get back up on your feet. If you work on that resolve, you will get used to those knockbacks and over time you will start to see those hard days as the *best* ones – because they are the days that *build* you and create the strength you need to move forwards. But this is getting ahead of myself, because no one feels this way at the beginning, and it takes a lot of perspective and hindsight to appreciate the value these trials bring to you.

Taking it all back to the beginning, when I was younger, I didn't really know what perseverance meant. I certainly wasn't conscious that I had persevered at anything. However, because of my condition and the philosophy according to which I was raised, there wasn't really a day of my life when I hadn't been persevering to achieve something, even if it might seem absolutely tiny from the outside. I have had to persevere at the same simple tasks again and again and again just in order to exist in an able-bodied world, and those tasks beat me *so many times*. I honestly couldn't count. But I kept coming back day after day. I never woke up and thought, that's it, I'll never make it, I might as well give up, because in my mind that would be letting my legs, my condition, the steps, the doctors, whoever thought I wouldn't amount to anything, win. Even when you feel you want to stop or you must stop, I always say come back the next day and give it another go.

LIFE SUCKS, PERSEVERANCE IS THE BEST DEFENCE

One of my key learnings is that the earlier you realize that life is just universally hard (for different people in different ways depending on their privileges), the easier it will be for you to cope with the inescapable setbacks that are coming your way. Even today life is hard! I don't mean that as a reflection of where I'm at, because that's all good, but more that it's physically hard every day. Yesterday I wanted to walk to get fish and chips with a friend, but it was such an effort. Hills, rocks, uneven ground – just every part of it was a pain in the butt. The pain it causes to my legs is so annoying, but you breathe in, suck it up and push through. What else am I going to do? Sit down and say, 'Hey, carry me, would ya?' No. I've never known any other way than to just put one foot in front of the other and get on with it. Of course, it's not only my mobility issues that make life hard, because we all have things that grind us down. Work is hard, relationships are hard, mental health is hard. Getting up in the morning can be hard. The world around you can feel hard with negativity and bad news and all sorts of scary and terrible messages to drag you down at every moment. Everywhere you look there is trouble and strife.

But as I said before, it sucks for *everyone*! Doors don't just open endlessly until you reach your ideal position in life and even for those who seem to have coasted to success, there will always be a blip in the story – that's just how it goes. I was recently at a graveyard, visiting a friend's relative. When I looked along those lines of stones, all I could think about was how much each individual had struggled in their lives. Struggled to make money, struggled to find peace within themselves, struggled to build a career, a family, a home. And now they're all just a name etched in stone. You stress all the way through your life, sometimes you're happy, sometimes you're not. And then it's done and you're just a name in a graveyard. I am sorry if my perception seems very bleak, but that is how I see it. Life is super, super short and super, super hard. You strive every day, but because of the ephemeral nature of life, you have to keep front of mind what you're striving for. Achieving your goals is an incredible feat, but you have to balance those ambitions with enjoying the ride too. These struggles have all come before and there are generations of people who toiled in a bid to make something of their lives – it's a story as old as time.

For me, there is no other option than to just push on. Constantly striving can feel like walking through quicksand or tar. Or a swamp. When everything feels like it's going against you, it's really hard to keep picking your feet up: you could give in to sinking at any moment. But if you stop, there is always the chance that you're going to drown. If I'm honest, after *every* racing season, I want to give up. Every single year, I finish and say, that's it, I'm done. I'm done! But then I'm never actually done. If I were to give up, it would be a decision based on all manner of factors, not just that I felt

I couldn't face the obstacles again in the moment. I have been through some hopeless times trying to secure sponsorship and I've explained how many doors I've had to knock on. Even now, it's a battle, one that can create a crisis of confidence.

It is, of course, possible to have some success which feels relatively straightforward. When you start out, you have no baggage, few expectations and a lot of beginner's motivation. When I began my racing career, everything was on an upward trajectory. I had nothing to prove and nothing to lose. Let's imagine I started on the first step of the ladder and I fell off. It wouldn't hurt, there wouldn't be any pain, because it's just a single step backwards. But when you progress and things stop going to plan, you can feel you've fallen down a whole flight of stairs, and that is rough. It *really* hurts, it can break you and you have to heal from that breakage and begin from a lower step again.

My first season was built off the back of a massive amount of unconscious perseverance. To me it felt like I was just getting on with my life and doing what I needed to do to be able to do the things I wanted. At the point where I was able to step in and out of a race car, I can admit that I felt untouchable and that I could pretty much do anything. It was great! Who wouldn't love that? I would say that the real, true, hard work for me didn't really start until after the first two years. That time on track was like a fairy-tale. Obviously, it wasn't easy and I was having to push myself in the gym and get through a lot of pain and inexperience, but on my personal barometer, it was a walk in the park, because I didn't have to do any additional work in terms of the commercial side of things. My dad handled all my sponsorship, he looked after the money, so all I had to do was turn up and drive.

It wasn't until that structure, the safety blanket, was all gone that it really hit hard. Because I was like, shit, I actually have to start from level one in understanding what my value is. Why would people buy into me or fund me, what makes me different, what sets me apart? The constant up and down, up and down, up and down is such a headfuck. One minute you think you're getting somewhere, the next minute you realize you're not at all. And then you have to continue to get through that period of time in order to keep driving upwards. Because if you stop then you'll never really know the end of the story.

In my career there have been many times when I could have just stopped. But if I had, I wouldn't be writing this book. If I had stopped and been like, meh, that didn't work out, I wouldn't have a career. So obviously I'm so happy that I didn't call it quits, even when things felt like they were too damn hard. Equally, a lot of it has been seriously *not fun*. For me, some of the hardest times are persevering when I know it's not working. When I'm hitting my head against a brick wall on a daily basis, sure that no matter what I do, it's not going to happen. If you can't see it working, you're like, what's the point? Will it ever work? That is just such a huge challenge and one that I know nearly every successful person has faced.

RE-EVALUATING YOUR GOALS IS NOT THE SAME AS QUITTING

There is this message that we should all know when to throw in the towel. That we should stop throwing good money after bad, stop flogging the proverbial dead horse. But the thing is, what you class as successful can shift and change with your experience. When I was younger, I measured success by my brother's achievements. Now obviously, I'm nowhere near as successful or talented as he is at driving a car. Nowhere near. And it doesn't have to be my brother, he's just the driver of our generation. Let's say I'm nowhere near as successful or talented as Michael Schumacher or Ayrton Senna. I will never be a seven times Formula 1 World Champion or a multi-millionaire and in the past that might have made me feel like a failure. But now I know that that reality doesn't mean I can't be successful within motorsport and successful on my own terms. That I can't be *a great success in my own eyes.*

What other people might see as middle of the road or even a waste of time can be life-changing and life-affirming for you. As long as you view what you are doing as something of value and something that you're proud of, that's a success. The fact that you gave it a go, even if it didn't work, is a success. Or if you gave it a go and it's reaping the rewards, it can still be a massive success. As long as what you are doing is giving you what you *need* from it – fulfilment, happiness or material or financial benefits – that's *more* than enough! That is all that matters. I think you should keep your towel until you personally *truly* believe it's time to throw it in. Only you can say when that is, and it may be never. You might not be performing to tens of thousands of people at the O2, but you could still be travelling the country singing. You might be on tour or at a local arena, getting paid to sing, and that might feel incredibly valuable to you. There is only one Beyoncé, so it's OK if that's not you.

Success is a mixture of achievement and acceptance. It's what you deem to be successful, and that moves over time as you learn to value yourself for both your assets and your shortcomings. It's about choosing to see the best side of every scenario. I might have had a really shit race and finished P20 and I'm pissed off and upset.

But on my in-lap to the pits, I'll start thinking, actually, I got a really great start, I made some awesome overtakes, I made the right decisions at the right time; I didn't make any mistakes and I placed ahead of my teammates. I'm where the car should be. That's a successful race. End of. But this is because I've made that decision for myself and looked at the bigger picture instead of focusing on the 19 cars that finished ahead of me. Success is all about your mindset.

I know first-hand that there is always another negative storyline I could dip into to describe my life and I could always choose to lean into a darker narrative. We all could. On a daily basis, I try to push it up back into the light, because I could absolutely be the victim and define myself and my life by its hardships, failures and fuck-ups. There is sometimes an edge to perseverance, because you can use it like a stick to beat yourself with. When you persevere, you fail at some point. But you can make a decision in terms of how you cope with that. If I can't control a challenge, I have to do my best to reframe it and turn it into a positive. If I can't do that, I need to implement some damage control and, as much as possible, stop any negatives from impacting my path. I sometimes feel like I'm on tenterhooks just waiting for the axe to fall again and that isn't the most relaxing way to live your life. But I do think that's the reality of what it feels like when you are walking the high road every single day, pushing, persevering to create something that seems so hard.

For me, one of the cornerstones of gratitude is embracing the darker side of the narrative. I like to share the journey and make sure that everyone knows I didn't just wake up and get here. So many people cover up the hard knocks that are part and parcel of any success and I am grateful that I have learned not to be like that, because it creates such unreasonable expectations. When you start with a challenge, you have to try to teach yourself to stay grounded and not to take anything for granted. It's a really fine balance. Even when life is great, you need to remember that it wasn't always this way and it might not be like it forever, so you should really take time to smell the roses. When life is tough, it's about remembering that it could be worse. A lot fucking worse.

HOW TO PERSEVERE WHEN THE RUG IS PULLED

I mentioned back in Lesson Four the big tumble I almost took in 2022 when my title sponsor pulled out and I was left with only a few days to turn things around. What I haven't shared was how that season was meant to be a massive break for me. The contract that was withdrawn was to be a Toyota factory driver, which was going to be a huge achievement and it was something I was incredibly excited about. It's a true example of feeling on top of the world and that things were finally going in the direction I had hoped for. But two weeks before the first race of the season, the sponsorship that I'd had for the previous three years was withdrawn and, as a result, my deal was pulled. I had only four or five days to find £150k or else I wouldn't be racing at all that year. I remember hanging up the phone after being told and just standing in the rain thinking, fuck, what now? That was a towel-throw moment if I've ever seen one.

But I knew I had to keep racing – at that juncture it was central to everything that I was building. I couldn't not be in a race car, because so much of the rest of what I was doing away from the track was connected to that. For about half an hour I had to go through the motions and emotions – the 'no one wants to sponsor you because you're shit', the 'you're worthless, no one cares or values you'. I let all those thoughts flood in – it's important to know that we all have those thoughts and that having negative thoughts doesn't mean you're going to fail or you're doing something wrong. It's how you deal with them that matters. I let my mind do its worst. I even stood in the corner of the room with my head facing the wall as I let those degrading thoughts race through my mind. I then took the deepest breath and decided it was time to come up with the next plan.

Over the next five days, all I did was sit at my desk and call every number and email every person I had ever met through my entire career who might be able to help me. The team I had left the season before said they still had a seat for me if I could raise the money, so the task was to get to that magic number. I hardly ate or slept, I just focused on following up on every single avenue I could think of. In the end, I scraped a huge chunk of it together, but still needed a little personal financial investment to get me over the line. It was now one week before the first race and I knew I owed it to myself to remain on that grid and show that, even after being let down and disregarded at the last minute, I was not going down without a fight. Also, I wanted to show that, because I believed in my business plan – my life plan – so much, I was even willing to put my own money in *again* to do it. It was gut-wrenching, but once I got there I sat and tapped myself on the chest so I could feel in my heart how proud I was of myself for sticking to my guns.

I'm going to be frank with you. I absolutely wouldn't want to do it again. I wouldn't wish that kind of experience on my worst enemy. But as much as I'd dread a rerun, I do know now that it wasn't impossible after all and that I have enough in my tank to persevere towards a goal even in the midst of total despair. I'm not sure that I believe perseverance is like a muscle, because you can't continuously build it to make it rock solid. Instead, I think it's about experience. Perseverance is built through knocking yourself right back down to dust. What I've found is that, as you go through life, you realize how much of your childhood and your formative experiences and traits remains relevant. What you experienced as a kid and the things you pushed through, you really can take that strength on into your adult life.

This is one of the reasons that I think overprotective parenting can really backfire, because you deprive your kids of these toils that get written into their backbones while they are young. At the end of the day in 2022, I got rejected and that felt exactly the same as being rejected as a kid. I can see now, from a higher level, how these things relate and connect to each other and the reason I managed to get through that time is that I have learned to deal with rejection. I know instinctively inside myself how I cope and how I move forwards.

I also know the steps I need to take to get out of the rejection phase and back to flexing my perseverance muscle. I first take myself away and go and listen to music to help me relax, totally alone. Then I start looking inwards and remind myself of my qualities and values. After an hour or so, I know I will begin to feel much better and be able to get myself mentally back on top, in order to reconnect with my tenacity. That is my personal process, and it might differ for you, but whenever it happens to me, I know how I can work myself to a more positive point. In some instances, that process has to be fast-tracked because you don't have a week or even a day to get back onto the perseverance train. Sometimes it is truly fight or flight, sink or swim. The anxiety around perseverance can be so deep and uncomfortable. I don't want to sugar-coat anything, because pushing yourself to the limits can feel like you're tearing yourself apart inside, while you run on adrenaline and cortisol to plug the dam against disaster. But if it's in aid of preserving something you really, *really* want and really, *really* believe in, it will be worth it, even if it's only to be able to say to yourself that you left it all in the ring even when the rug was pulled from beneath.

PERSEVERANCE IS A MENTALITY, NOT A FIXED-END GOAL

Another thing to consider is that even when you do achieve things, perseverance means you keep pushing beyond your original targets. As you tick off the original goals, you will probably make more, because that is the nature of ambition: the horizon keeps moving further away the closer you get to it. Perseverance is basically the engine that keeps you moving forwards on your journey through life and stops you from ever giving up. I have achieved so much and come so far, and if I'm honest I do worry about the idea that I will never get to the 'end' or find full contentment. When I look at my dad, I see a man who will never retire. He's not looking for a comfortable chair *ever* and I know that both my brother and I take after him. I love that and I hate it at the same time. I love it because I wouldn't be as strong as I am if I didn't have the drive that Dad has passed down to me. It's an incredible blessing to have. But to have that drive which constantly keeps you pushing and pushing and never backing down . . . I'm always at full throttle, never just taking a few weeks to take my foot off the gas . . .

There is definitely a worry that I'm never going to feel that I've completed or achieved *anything*. I do sometimes wish I could say, great, I've done enough, I'm happy to sit back and chill now. But that's not me. I've turned motorsport and disability in sport on its head, I've done everything and more than achieved my original goals. I never fully understood what it felt like to come across the line and feel a true sense of achievement, but my P6 at Donington Park at the start of 2023 really changed that. Now I've experienced that success, I just want more. It's the most satisfying feeling I've ever had in my life and it does feel like a drug, for sure. That sense of complete bliss and self-acceptance is something I would love to feel again and I will continue to strive for it. But if I don't get to experience it again, that's OK too. I'm grateful I experienced it at least once.

Either way, it will probably never be enough. I'll sit in my car at the next race at Thruxton, stressed to my eyeballs, thinking, how am I going to get as much performance as possible from this car? For me that is part and parcel of passion and if I was sitting in the car and not really caring about the competitive element of it or getting the very best out of the race weekend, *that* would be the time to start to think about doing something else.

In better news, I think it's also worth saying that if you do persevere for long enough, you are going to see results somewhere down the line and obviously results in themselves can be incredibly motivating. Your efforts might not lead exactly to where you imagined, but something positive will come from them somewhere, at some point. Looking back on all the steps you've taken to reach your goals and everything that has gone into each and every one of your achievements builds such a huge amount of self-respect and worth.

But again, it doesn't mean you have to push as hard as I do to be happy or content, because I know very well that you can be both with and without grandiose goals and still find both to be elusive at times. We are all so different. One of my best friends always jokes that I should keep lowering my expectations until my life matches my goals. He says that's what he does, but whether he *actually* does it I am not sure. Either way he seems to be happy with where he's at in life. I'm sure he has goals, passions and desires, but he is not getting stressed about anything, he's just content and thinks what will be will be.

While I am often happy, contentment is a tricky piece of the puzzle for me. Part of me thinks you can't be a Hamilton and be content at the same time. If we were content with where we were at, Lewis wouldn't have won so many world titles, he would have stopped at one. He wouldn't still be racing now trying to get his eighth. My dad would be sitting back right now having a lovely life with all the success he has built for himself. I think the truth is that you can't have headline success without there being some kind of cost. And for us, it's somewhat true that contentment has been the price. I can't speak for my parents or Lewis – perhaps they are actually far more content than me – but I just know that it's the Hamilton nature to always strive for more.

HOW TO KEEP GOING WHEN THE HONEYMOON PERIOD IS OVER

Lots of people tell me that they struggle to persevere with their goals. Often, they say they start really strong, but over time they find the whole thing becomes less exciting and motivating and they lose their resolve. Many people believe they just don't have the ability to persevere long term. My natural reaction is to look at the reason you feel that way. Is it because you have taught yourself that you give up? It's not that you were born a quitter, no one was. But as we discussed previously, your words make your reality, so if you keep giving up, you haven't allowed yourself to grow or get uncomfortable and that is vital to finding the potential to persevere. You won't know until you do it once, until you go through the feeling of not giving up and of coming out the other side. That one day when you tell yourself you're not going to quit and then it works out . . . you're like, shit, this is what Nic has been talking about. On that day you will find that you gain so much strength and so much power through overcoming not just an obstacle in your way but also your own mental barrier – the barrier you had created in your mind.

Don't get me wrong, it's not like I'm a paragon of virtue and I have totally had times in my life when my perseverance has failed me. There have been eras when I've given up on overcoming challenges and obstacles. There have been times when I've given up on myself. I'm not sitting on any high horse – whatever you have done, however much you might feel disappointed in yourself, I have been there too. I've probably been way, way lower. Constantly persevering and striving is so incredibly draining, especially when you don't see any progress. It can be physically and mentally destroying. You could be spending all your energy every single day for months and getting absolutely nothing back. It can feel like you're pouring your energy, your life, down the drain. And with every knock you take, your energy reserves deplete and you can't go back in with the same vigour. Seeing who you are and what you really want when you get to the bottom of the tank is incredibly revealing. Who are you when you're on your back? It's like being knocked out in a boxing ring and you've got that countdown from ten. You get to one and you're out, you've expelled everything you had, you've punched as hard as you possibly could and you've lost. But how you get up tells you a lot about who you are.

It's totally OK to be counted out. If you get counted down to one because you can't get up, it's OK to accept that *in that moment* you have nothing left. You gave it your all and you can be so proud of that. It's OK! Sometimes you are up against something too big or strong for you. But just because you can't do it *right now* doesn't mean you will be in the same position forever. *In this moment* you are being taught that you have to take one step back to take two steps forwards. Just because you tapped out doesn't mean you can't come back stronger. You can recover and gain the strength and positivity to have another go later down the line. Maybe that's an hour from now, a week from now, a year from now. Either way, you can always give it another shot. There is a difference between accepting that you're not yet up to the task and simply giving up. You can be honest that you aren't prepared yet, you're not ready. Let me go home, invest my time and energy, and I'll come back when I'm ready. It's having that strength to hold your hands up and say this isn't working right now.

I don't believe that the spiral down to rock bottom I had in my twenties was inevitable. Knowing what I know now I can see how it could have been stopped. Today I understand that there is no shortcut to success, no shortcut to financial security, or wealth, or growth. The rejections that I've encountered along the way weren't personal, it was just business. How you feel in the moment is part of life's process, but it doesn't necessarily mean that you have to accept every element of that because you can keep fighting and keep going. You have to think of the long game and seek the bigger picture.

PERSEVERANCE VS. DESPERATION

When you are head down, pushing so hard towards a goal, it is really easy to become blinkered and continue along a line of attack that simply isn't working. In that case, your thirst for the end point can really ignore you to the error of your ways. One of the worst things that I did was make decisions through desperation. Ideally you never want to be in that position. Decisions should be calculated, and we should all be taught that making any decision out of desperation lets yourself down. If you're making decisions out of desperation you're not prepared, you're not looking at the picture clearly and you're not considering any other options that might help you to reach the final point. An element of perseverance is being true to yourself and getting to your goals in your own way.

In the past, I have made decisions that looked like good moves from the outside and meant I had something to tell my friends and family and post on Instagram. But they were actually *desperate* moves. I was trying and trying to make something – anything – of my life and I have to give myself credit for that. But it was all through desperation and I was making all the wrong choices, all the wrong business decisions, working with the wrong teams, the wrong sponsors, building the wrong relationships and then reacting in a terrible way to certain things in a total panic. If something didn't go my way, I didn't step back, regroup and look at a new plan. I just kept ploughing ahead, without really thinking about the parts of me I was compromising to get there. That's not perseverance, that's just foolishness.

I knew I couldn't continue going in these different directions because nothing I was doing was working. So, I made a concerted effort to take a step back and stop being so desperado for something, anything, to work. What was really important in that moment was that my desire and passion for where I wanted to end up in my career never wavered. I still had this goal, but I knew that I had to come at it from a different angle and break away from what I was currently doing in order to find the new path. It's like being an alcoholic and holding your hands up to having a problem and then rebuilding who you are root and branch to find a new way of living. It isn't quitting to say I need help, I need to stop walking this road, this isn't working. Having that strength and self-actualization makes you a stronger person because you cannot thrive in denial.

Some people believe that perseverance is throwing mud at a wall and hoping something sticks. Of course, throwing anything is trying and that is always to be encouraged. But if you really want to achieve your goals, you need to direct your perseverance and energy in the *right direction*. That is really what your late teens and early twenties are all about – finding that clear vision to make a calm, cool and collected step-by-step plan to get to where you want to be unhindered by self-sabotage or a lack of self-esteem. You cannot see that holistic critical path when you have no experience. You cannot approach setbacks along that path without taking it personally until you learn the *huge* role that failure plays in success. I cannot judge myself as a 20-year-old from the vantage point of being in my thirties with all the experience and success I have now. Everything that I have learned over the past 10 or 15 years has shaped how I react to every little thing that comes my way today. It's unrealistic to suggest that you're just going to step into a business straight out of school and not feel out of your depth and desperate sometimes. That you won't not throw mud at a wall.

The reason I'm able to talk about it now is that I have thrown mounds and heaps and hills of mud at every wall and watched it not stick and instead just *sliiiide* slowly downwards. And from that, I've learned to change my technique. Perhaps today I throw at a slightly different angle. Or I build up with mud from the ground. Of course, just because it sticks once doesn't mean it will always stay there. You can never guarantee that your next handful of mud will reach its target. But the fact you at least have something to work from makes all the difference.

YOU NEVER ACTUALLY GO BACK TO SQUARE ONE

Whenever you are on an upward trajectory, it feels like everything is sticking and your rise will last forever, but it doesn't mean that it can't all come crashing down – because it really can. And then you get to the truly important moment. Not giving up in that painful bit, when you feel like you are literally back at the foot of the hill, is one of the hardest and most fundamental moments in the perseverance journey and something that nearly every successful person will talk about. What I now know is that when it feels like you're back at square one, you rarely are. Yes, it might feel like you've lost it all and everything you have worked for was for nothing. It was so awful when I had to restart my career and yes, it 100 per cent felt like it was from zero. But it wasn't actually zero. Sure, things might initially feel a little familiar, but you are starting with so much knowledge in the bank. You have all these tools and weapons to go back into war with. You also have learned which tool to use for which task because you have completed your apprenticeship and you're ready for every challenge. It makes the whole thing so much easier on both mental and physical levels.

Once you get the ball rolling again, you can maintain the momentum without any desperation. It will be quicker to make the same moves, it won't require so much perseverance. Yes, you have baggage, but your rucksack is full of these useful tools. Before, when everything started falling away, I didn't even realize I was falling; I didn't see any of it coming. But here's the thing: you can't know everything, especially at the beginning. Pain, lessons, grief, stress and hopeful failures and fiascos are coming your way, but if you do manage to keep going, you will have learned to leapfrog all of them and will eventually make it to the final square on the board.

PERSEVERANCE OUTSIDE OF WORK

Of course, perseverance isn't just about work and professional achievement. I've spoken a lot about career in this chapter, but I also use my skills of perseverance in nearly every element of my life, notably the work I do on myself.

I have often been asked why I keep going to therapy and if I will ever stop. What I've realized by persevering with my sessions is that when things are going really well, therapy helps you to not fuck it up. The work I do in therapy has been fundamental to me, and because we all evolve and shift so much in ourselves over the years, I don't see it as something that needs an end. For me it is an eternal thing, a space for hope and self-exploration, so I budget it into my life. Twice a week from now until forever . . . *I hope*. I have been going to my sessions while writing this book, which has helped me learn more and more about myself and hopefully will help those reading it too.

With all due respect, I have no need for any feedback on this lifestyle choice. I understand it is a privilege to be able to afford it and I wish wholeheartedly that everyone who needs it could have access to mental healthcare as and when they need it. But when it comes to people saying that someone has become 'reliant' on therapy and 'doesn't have the strength' to live without it, I just roll my eyes. People go to church every Sunday, or else they spend their money on football tickets and find their faith and sense of self in the stands. No one is calling them out for being over-dependent on the thing that gives them strength and peace in their life. So why is therapy such a trigger for so many people? At the end of the day, this is what works for me, keeps me strong in both my mind and my spirit and keeps me focused on the upswing and positive stories from my life. To me it is indispensable and, uncomfortable as it sometimes gets, it's something I will continue to persevere with.

Similarly going deep into relationships and continuing to work tirelessly at romantic, plutonic and family ties are things I see as a lifelong challenge. When you are in it for the long run, relationships take a *lot* of work. You are going to want to quit all the time. This is another aspect of life that I believe our social media apps and the media in general really skew for us. Finding happiness with your partner isn't something that is easy or that you can ever take for granted. When you see these perfect loving relationships online, you have to remember that you're only seeing a sliver of what really goes on, stripped bare of the work, persistence and resolve that go into maintaining a healthy and positive union. Instagram and TikTok and the rest of them can be fantasies and even when you see something that looks legit, you have to question *why* someone has posted it for everyone else to see. It's very easy to get caught up with ideas and expectations for things that don't really exist. So many of us are comparing ourselves to others in this zero-sum game. OK, they might be happy. That's possible. But it's equally possible they are miserable and just shared a happy picture to paper over their own cracks. There is no lie-o-meter on social media and even though we kind of know it, so many of us end up believing what we see.

So often I'm told that the early days of a relationship, at least before you get married, should feel easy, like brushing your teeth. My take on that is if you have a relationship without any tension or challenges, then you are most likely not connecting on a deep and meaningful level because that shit is *hard*. You are not going deep enough to do the work that you both need to do to really find each other and know whether or not you have a happy future together. Every boyfriend and every girlfriend grind each other's gears at some point. Scratch that, any two people in such close proximity, spending so much time together, will have some level of conflict, even if it's handled very respectfully and calmly. No relationship is perfect, no person is perfect, so if a relationship is meaningful, you will be fighting with each other and for it until the end. I'm not saying it's going to be catastrophic hurricane-level rows every day. I mean more that you will have difficult periods and have to weather storms to persevere with your relationship.

So many people struggle with their relationships, but if you want to improve them, you have to first look into yourself and think how you can be a better partner, friend, son, daughter, father, mother, brother or sister. Through trying to improve my romantic relationships, I have learned so much about myself, things that will stay with me for the rest of my life. In the past, there have been parts of my relationship where I made mistakes and took actions that didn't reflect my true feelings; that was because I was insecure and was internally questioning whether I was strong enough to be a partner, manly enough to be a boyfriend. I had all these thoughts about myself, but I believed it meant that I was too emotional and I needed to suppress my tears. By reading a lot of literature around masculinity and heterosexual relationships, I have really had my eyes opened. After spending hours trying to understand things about both myself as an individual and myself within relationships, I am now in such a stronger position.

As I've mentioned before, one of the biggest things that my mental health journey has helped me with is putting boundaries in place. When you get to the point where you really feel a relationship isn't working, you have to ask yourself if you have given it your best shot. It's very easy to think, yeah, of course I did, I was amazing, they were just awful and toxic. I did this and that while they did that and this. Blah, blah, blah. But what if you really step back and ask yourself, how much did your actions benefit your partner? How much did you help your partner grow? Did you always say the right things, did you make decisions considering their feelings, or were you quite selfish in a lot of areas? Were you clear about your needs from the outset? If they stepped over the line, had you even told them it was there? People aren't mind-readers. Often, if you do a lot of soul searching, you will realize that you weren't quite as amazing as you thought you were.

This is all more hard work and, let's be honest, *no one* likes home truths. But a relationship is never going to be all about you: you go into a relationship to give. You can't exclusively take from the other person and have it on your own terms unless you are truly selfish. You have to give a part of yourself to somebody and that stands for any kind of relationship from business to friendship to romance.

The more you can stay open-minded when things aren't going well, the more you will be able to reflect and use self-criticism to come to a real conclusion about your compatibility for the long term. Sure, a relationship might be toxic and sometimes people are just not meant to be together. It can be easier to say it's too hard, it's not right, I need to just move on; it's not worth the fight. But in those situations, when you realize that you didn't actually do everything you needed to do to make it a good relationship, you will always have a question mark hanging over it. Knowing I hadn't done everything that I could have would always have made me look back with regret. Just like with your career and your dreams, you should only tap out when you've left everything in the ring. *Then* you make your decision.

At the moment, many of my personal relationships are in a period of transition. This all comes back to boundaries. In general, people don't like it when you put boundaries in place or try to change the dynamic in a relationship. Showing that you mean what you say can really put people out. Now I have more respect for myself and my own values and what I will and won't tolerate with people, I'm experiencing a lot of pushback; that often feels like a massive drag and some days I just *wish* I could wash my hands of the whole thing. But overall, I'm far calmer and more thoughtful when I approach any kind of conflict. I don't argue anywhere near as much and that has helped me stay in the game with even the most difficult of relationships.

The fact that people in my life have commented about the change in the way I relate to them means that they are now seeing the shift in action. When I say something, I mean it and I now know my true value. Eventually, my relationships will be better than they have ever been. But it is a process, and you have to keep going with your boundaries even when people make you feel guilty, or make you question yourself for putting them in place. That's all come from finding my self-respect. I disrespected myself for years by allowing people to trample all over me and it takes time, experience and maturity to be able to see that. You have to accept that not everyone is going to be able to continue walking beside you as you shed your old skin. But if it was a meaningful relationship and that person finds you add value to their life, they will come back eventually. All of this can be really close to home in that it can lead to disagreements with your best friends, parents and siblings. Saying, 'No, I don't appreciate that' to your closest humans can be tough. Speaking up in this way is really a big challenge. But sticking to your guns with this new way of relating to the people you love is the best way to build your self-respect and value for yourself.

Takeaways

* Keep reminding yourself that reaching your goal isn't likely to happen overnight. Goal achievement is a process, and the number-one factor in its success isn't talent or luck – it's how much you are able to persevere. There is no magic wand, it's just staying power. Hold tight, you will get there . . . in the end.
* No one was born a quitter; you weren't born with a tendency to give up on things. That is behaviour that you have learned over time and has probably become a self-fulfilling prophecy as you have gone through your life. Because you have quit in the past, it's easier to quit today. That's just what you do, right? Wrong. It's what you *have*

done, but you don't have to do it any more. Keep saying to yourself all day long, 'I am going to persevere' or 'I will not quit' as a mantra and the energy those words generate will change your whole perspective. Equally, be wary of telling yourself that you can't cut it. That is a choice, not an innate character quality.

* Putting any of this advice into action may change the dynamics of your relationships and this is where learning to be clear about your boundaries comes into play. It can be hard for some people to watch others change their story and they can struggle to let go of the person they knew and the relationship as it was. Stay firm with what you expect from people and the real friends will adapt with you. This can be hard, *but you've got this*. Remember, you can't hold on tight to the past while you step into the future. You have to make an intentional decision about where you want to go and *stick to it* like your life depends on it. No excuses, no compromises. Tomorrow is a brand new day.

AFTERWORD: SO, NOW THAT I HAVE YOUR ATTENTION

It's a funny thing, writing a book, because you're the person doling out advice, you're supposed to be the expert and yet I have learned so much from the writing too. Life, especially one navigating adversity, can feel like it goes from one battle to the next and when you're constantly focused on the next hurdle, it can be hard to connect with the here and now. If you have these big goals and dreams and see life as a game of snakes and ladders, you rarely take the time to say, wow, that was an incredible moment or achievement, because your eyeline is always set to the horizon. Reading my words back has been the ultimate reminder that we *all* have so much wisdom inside us, we just need to listen to our instincts, have a little faith and give ourselves credit where it is due. After everything I said in the introduction about my story not being special or me not being particularly notable, this book has given me pause and made me realize that perhaps in that sense I've got the wrong end of the stick.

I've never ever watched myself give a speech, so this is really the first time I have heard my own words, almost as a member of the audience. Even though it's my story, I haven't *lived* every moment. I haven't always been fully present for everything that has happened to me, I've just been driving forwards, often with my gaze locked on the ground. Now, it's like, oh yeah, shit, that did happen and that was *awesome*! I did just decide I was going to walk one day and I made that happen. I did aim to make history in motorsport and I did it several times. I did promise myself I would get out of the deepest hole of depression and financial self-abuse and, while it's taken years to get here, I *have* in some senses arrived. I aimed to overcome my fears and here I am.

It's the first time I've taken in my experiences from this perspective and I think it has made me view myself slightly differently. I started this book saying that people would only be interested in reading a book about extraordinary people like my brother, not about someone like me. I hadn't achieved enough, hadn't done this, hadn't done that. But writing this book has proved to me that that isn't true. I am impactful in my own way. I do have something to say and my voice has a power. That voice, who I am, what I've been through and what I continue to go through every day are *worthy* of attention. That realization has taught me in turn to be even more open, because scraping my soul of its memories has reminded me that there are extraordinary things to be found in even the most mundane of experiences, which even people like me, who don't immediately command consideration, go through. It isn't only conventionally beautiful or super-smart or extreme winners who deserve attention, it's *all of us*.

What I've discovered is that I've been juggling all these different balls over the years in order to feel better about myself. Because when it comes down to it, I hadn't felt that anything I'd done in my life was good enough. It's almost like I needed a piece of paper or money or a medal to prove to the world that I didn't deserve to live my whole life in the shadows. All these stories have been about me trying to achieve some kind of validation or notoriety when I was desperate, when I was going in 15 different directions at once. Even when I was so badly bitten by trying to make something of myself. I've taken so many leaps that haven't worked out. Everybody hates themselves in those moments, and it takes some serious distance to stop torturing yourself with regrets. I wish I hadn't done many of the things I've done or made so many mistakes, and I probably would be in a better place at least on some levels if I hadn't. But also, what are you meant to do? The past is the past, life is what it is. Dust it off, go again.

The experiences I have shared with you here are all based on the hard-won lessons that life has served me. If you see all the tests that your life sends your way as arrow guiders to learn something more about yourself, it can give you a little bit of reassurance even as you flounder under their weight. Now when a trial comes my way – as I've said before in this book, struggle is always just around the corner – I do deal with it very differently. I don't catastrophize. I know, based on my record, that it *will* most probably be fine. Getting to know yourself and finding this level of confidence to steer through these difficult moments is the work of a lifetime.

Now that I'm in my early thirties I am slowly starting to see the fruits of my labours and it's funny how many things are beginning to make sense. I can see so clearly that things I went through when I was 12 or 21 are feeding directly into a decision or situation I'm dealing with today. It's like we are all a cumulation of our experiences, so however awful they might be, they are also precious. I now know that my voice is *worth* something and that *I am* too. As I watch good things unfold around me, things that I value and deem as successes, I'm like, wow, man, I'm so proud! This is so cool. The work has started to pay off, often in ways I had never imagined, but it's all good. My only job now is to be grateful for the positive days, to feel proud of who I am and what I've built, and to stay strong in my passions and mental health for the days when the tides will, hopefully only temporarily, turn.

I have gained a lot from reliving my experiences here too. Not all of it has been comfortable; actually it's been incredibly painful at times. But seeing it all here, laid out, makes me think how fortunate I've been to find the strength to come out the other side. Of course, there have been moments when I've wished things could be easier. Even last night, I was thinking what a *drag* it is being disabled all the goddamn time. As much as I've overcome so many of my physical limitations and I'm chilled and centred with it, I do still find it so *bloody* annoying. It's like . . . now what? Last night, I kept catching my foot and stepping backwards and falling off balance. *Whyyyy*? Why am I so off balance today? What happened since yesterday? It's so frustrating sometimes!

The difficult truth is that you cannot complete disability the way you complete a computer game. It will always be there to humble and challenge you. Yes, you can manage it to the best of your abilities. Stuff around your condition that used to really get to you will not get to you any more. You can take the things you've learned from your condition into other areas of your life and that can completely change your trajectory in the most positive of ways. I always have that voice in the back of my head: if you can overcome your condition, then you can do *anything*. Even in the depths of my despair, that message still rang true and helped pull me back from the abyss.

At other times, it has given me a huge amount of confidence to face other challenges because it was just such a big win. But it's all still ongoing. I'm not saying that my disability has been my only challenge, but if, for example, we look at my experience with my finances, which was *the* lowest time of my life, that is now completed. I am not going back there. However horrendous it was, it is over. My disability will *never* be over, I will die with my condition, so I can't put it to bed. As I sit here writing, I'm raging because one of my ribs has popped out, my pelvis is stiff, my neck is aching *and* I'm on a holiday so I'm going to have to swallow that pain for a week. I've come to terms with the fact that I'll never be *free* of it, but I'm not a saint: it *still* pisses me off.

This book has also given me clarity on how isolated and lonely I have been through times in my life. I know that many young people experience a similar sense of alienation, especially if they feel excluded from places and spaces and can't see a future for themselves in society because of innumerable issues which might be evident, or alternatively might be going on inside their mind. Not fitting in anywhere and feeling it is only you who is having thoughts like yours makes you feel like an alien. Telling everyone how I feel about that has taken a huge weight off my shoulders. Some of these pages will be hard for my friends and family to read, and I know they will say, well, you're not alone, you've always got us. And I do know that they are there for so much. But being able to explain that no matter what they do, there will still always be a barrier that can't be crossed and that I will always be alone with my physical challenges and their mental consequences feels freeing. It's not their fault, it's not my fault. It just is.

I am aware that this is not an entirely *happy* book. When my friends have said that they can't wait to read it, I've been slightly apprehensive, because some of it is just *so* much. It's going to be sticky and gnarly and even people who are really close to me and have known me since I was a child are going to be taken aback. I guess that is another lesson. We can never know *everything* about the people we love. The cold truth is that we are alone inside our minds, and no one can join us with whatever is going on in there. The sooner we come to terms with that and the sooner we take responsibility for it, the better. On the flipside, of course, there are lots of awesome and triumphant moments in this book too. It hasn't been some relentless nightmare, *has it?* There have been passages that have made me *absolutely* laugh my head off and punch the air with excitement and pride. I hope you didn't find it too gloomy, but I guess, that is real life. It's not all roses, is it?

As much as my family have supported me so much through my whole life, this does feel like a pinch-me moment of professional vindication too. For all the times that even they tried to guide me in a different direction, seeing my book on sale reminds me that keeping true to my own instincts and taking a lonelier path was the right choice. I know they finally get it now and can see all the pieces of my puzzle coming together. Hopefully this book has helped their understanding even more.

It has been so crazy to hold my book, to see it available online, to know that it's real, because this whole career feels like a fantasy, like something I imagined inside my mind. Well, I did imagine it, but to make it a reality is something I never thought would happen. That I have made an impact to this extent, on my own, is blowing my mind. Mine and Lewis's stories are obviously so different, but it's amazing that we have both, in our own ways, in our own relative contexts, achieved so much. All credit, of course, to our parents because I hold them responsible for so much, but we have both been a part of it too.

One thing that has become a running theme in this book is conversations around masculinity, which wasn't something that I had ever considered too deeply before I started writing and I certainly hadn't anticipated that it would be something I would explore so thoroughly. I want *everyone*, male or female, gay, straight or anything else, to be able to connect here, but I have realized that my particular lens has something to add to the conversations that so many people are having around modern masculinity and the crisis many young males are going through at this point in our history. As a disabled man, your masculinity is always in question and while the conclusions I've come to in this book go way beyond the disabled experience, the fact that I am disadvantaged physically gives me a keen eye for those traditional standards of manhood. I can see clearly why so many men are struggling and why we have such a tough time forging our identities. There are constant pressures which I feel every day. I feel I need to be seen as a strong man, a successful man, a loyal man. A man who is good in business and can provide for a family. But I also need to be a man who is incredibly supportive as a partner and one day as a father and husband. A man who is empathetic and kind, yet never weak or fragile. There is so much expectation and responsibility. Some of the characteristics which we are meant to have up our sleeves are the exact opposites of each other, and I think we need to be honest and say that no one person can encompass every single one of the facets supposedly required to be a 'good man' these days.

As for the fragility, guess what? Real men cry. Real men can be soft and emotional. That doesn't mean we can't be strong along other fault lines too. There are so many people, both men and women, who define masculinity as brute strength, who believe good men can never *falter* in their feelings. This is so incredibly toxic. The narrative of the stiff upper lip is so dangerous and it's one of the reasons that male suicide levels, especially among our youngest, are so high. Seventy-four per cent[5] of suicides in the UK are among men, over three times higher than for women. It's also the biggest cause of death in young males,[6] though suicide is most prevalent among mature men, aged 45–64. The culture of *manning up* and the stigma attached to admitting any kind of struggle have played a long-running part in this gender gap and if I can do anything to encourage other men just to talk through some of their feelings, I always will.

Living up to the standards of being 100 per cent tough at all times can, I have learned, make you incredibly vulnerable. As many as 40 per cent of men[7] have never spoken to *anyone, ever* about their mental health and the same percentage say that they would only do so if they were *seriously considering taking their own lives*. This is such an extreme situation, and so many men are missing out on support that they could have accessed earlier on in their mental health experience if they hadn't felt it was taboo. So many men are scared to open up, because they are scared about where it will go. Of course, women have mental health battles too, but the context remains different – they're meant to be emotional, after all. However, this does not make it OK.

I just think we can all agree that it's time to find a middle ground when it comes to masculinity and I hope that by the time you've got to this point in the book, you can see where I'm coming from. Yes, we should be taught to develop drive and self-sufficiency and passion. But we should also be taught to be kind to ourselves and that there is no shame in struggling. In this book I've spoken about my own experiences with depression, addiction and suicidal thoughts. I've also spoken about my athletic achievements, how I've defied the physical expectations of every doctor and expert and how I'm one of very few disabled people in the world competing against able-bodied people. Both things can be true at the same time. I am tough and I manage daily pain with true grit, but I also struggle sometimes and need support to even my keel. That doesn't make me less strong. We have got to leave that rubbish back in the Stone Age where it belongs. In this life, I have been so low, but I have also come back up for air. That is what strength is, not just breezing through life as if you're on a water slide.

You already know that I don't see myself as a hero or anything super special, but I have done all right and I'm still doing all right in tough circumstances. I've got to continue pushing and moving forwards, because I still haven't achieved everything I want to in my life. This journey of ups and downs has been, at times, heart-breaking. It's not like I'm sitting here feeling proud of sharing my battles with online gambling, for example. I *hate it,* I hate reading it and I'm so annoyed at myself for putting myself in that position to start with. But at the same time I'm also very grateful to have gone through it. It's a complicated thing. In writing this book, I've had to relive a lot of things that I wish had *never* happened to me. But then I think, on the other hand, if everything had worked out swimmingly all the way through, this would be a bit of a boring book, wouldn't it? What wisdom would I have to pass on? How much empathy would I have developed if I'd never laboured or been knocked down or had my dreams crushed? Who could I possibly help?

I know I'm not at the end of the tunnel, in fact I'm nowhere near out of the weeds. *I'm only 32,* for crying out loud! My condition will keep me in the weeds forever. But it's knowing now that I've got the tools to rumble through the jungle that makes all the difference. I still have work to do to release many feelings and emotions that continue to bubble up from within. But I am getting there, I really am, and that is something worth putting down on paper.

Don't tell my publishers, but I would have written this book for free. This project hasn't been about any material gain for me, *at all*. Yes, I've earned some money doing it and, as we all know, money isn't easy to make, but I'm not trying to cash in on anything. This book is about amplifying my *voice* and maximizing the attention it receives, because that's how I can help more people, simple as that. Sure, I can get paid for my time writing, or doing my speeches. I've got to eat; I've got to make my living. That's basic. But my intention and motivation to do it come from the belief that *this* is what I was sent here to do, this is my *mission*. If this book touches hundreds or thousands of people and has the chance to help change their lives, that to me is something priceless.

I am so incredibly proud *of* my brother and I'm so proud to *be* his brother and I wouldn't change any of that for the world. In my eyes, he is the most amazing person on the planet and I love him dearly. But having a sibling who is really well known (let alone arguably the best human to ever race a car) can become such a big part of your identity. I do hope that reading this book changes the perception on that, because I do have my *own identity* too and my *own voice*. And apparently, I have a lot to say with it! I'm not just Lewis's little brother with CP. I'm *more* than both my disability and who I'm related to and I believe I have lots to offer beyond those two facts of my birth.

I know voices like mine aren't heard that often and I hope that the book has offered a bit of an education in what people with disability go through, even though of course our challenges are all so varied and layered. I haven't sugar-coated anything, so I hope it offers a window into a space which is something hushed away. In this book, for once, I'm not trying to beat anyone or win. I'm not trying to be anything or prove myself to *anyone*. I'm just trying to *help* people. But in order to do that, I've had to come to the place where I believe that what I have to share is valuable. That I'm valuable. I know better than anyone that you can't force people to see their own worth, but I really hope that some of my words on these pages help you to start on the journey of self-discovery and self-worth, if that's something you struggle with too. *If I can, you can.*

AFTERWORD: LINDA

My waters broke when I was 31 weeks pregnant. I was meant to be on a train into work in London and instead I went into labour. It was a difficult birth and Nic was taken away immediately because he wasn't breathing – I actually didn't get to see him for two days, as he was on a ventilator. You don't expect to meet your baby in an incubator, and I just remember how tiny he looked: he was only 4lb 4oz – about 1.7kg. Nic was then in intensive care for five weeks and I didn't really hold him for about a month, which was obviously difficult. It was my first experience of motherhood (Lewis is biologically my husband Anthony's son, but not mine) and I had absolutely no frame of reference. If I'm honest, it's all a blur of sleepless nights and worry – I can't really put my finger on the details.

When we finally got Nic home, I was concerned, of course, because he was still so small. But as I hadn't been to any ante-natal classes – I had been working full time and hadn't expected him to arrive for another couple of months – I really didn't have anything to compare the experience or his development to. I didn't have a clue. As he grew and reached the sitting-up stage, around six months, I did notice that he was a bit wobbly, but I thought that was just a normal part of learning. We never thought that anything was really untoward until he was around one year old. By that point, he could pull himself up, but he was always on his tiptoes – he could never put his foot flat. I did think that wasn't quite right. Then when I put him in a walking frame, I noticed he moved backwards in it and that both his legs went at the same time – he couldn't move one leg independently of the other.

Eventually, when Nic was about 18 months, we had a meeting with a consultant. They did a lot of tests and we found out that Nic had some water around his brain, which scared me to death. While the consultant said we shouldn't worry so much about that as it would dissipate over time, he broke the news that Nic had what they called spastic diplegia. The prognosis was that he might never walk and at best he would need a walking stick. He also would need physiotherapy for the rest of his life. There was nothing more the consultant could say. And that was it. We were sent off, without any additional guidance, nothing to help us as parents, no support groups or anything in the way of education around Nic's condition. No ideas about what might happen over the years, how other people with the condition were impacted or the range of potential treatments ahead. It was really just go home and get on with it.

Fortunately, Anthony and I are live-in-the-moment kind of people. I don't spend a lot of time looking to the future and I deal with whatever is happening in front of my face. So that's what we did. We took Nic to his physio, did our best and tried to explore ways in which we could make his condition better than it sounded. The thing is, Nic was developing well in every other area. He was the loveliest, most engaged child, he just had issues with his fine motor skills, and as he got older his legs got tighter and tighter.

It's hard to remember how I felt during those years. When Nic was young, Lewis had started racing and was go-karting every weekend. Both Anthony and I were working full time, so every morning during the week, I'd drop Nic off at nursery and then Lewis at his childminder on my way to the station. Friday nights would be planning and packing for the weekend away, either in the UK or in Europe, as Lewis raced a lot in Italy too. We had a mobile home which we drove to the race circuits and there was never any time to sit at home and dwell, because we were always on the road. Inevitably, although we went to the race circuits as a family, Anthony was with Lewis working on the go-kart and I was with Nic doing our thing around and about the circuits.

But as Nic came towards puberty, worries did creep in, worries about what his life would look like as an adult. When he was younger, I would just scoop him up and off we would go. He couldn't walk, but that was as far as it went. Physically there was a lot of carrying and when you have a disabled child you realize how inaccessible our world really is to those who have different needs. When he was younger, Nic had a squint that he needed an operation for at Moorfields Eye Hospital in London. Getting him into London and then across the city on the tube was a huge challenge. At the time, I had a McLaren buggy for disabled children, and I had to carry him in that, up and down endless flights of stairs. There were so many moments like this when you had to take a deep breath and steel yourself, because that was just the way it was. I couldn't do anything about it.

We explored a range of treatment options, but at the time money was really tight, so it wasn't like we could just go and see that expert or this expert – it was all so expensive. In the end, we managed to do some fundraising to get him over to Hungary to the Conductive Education Centre. The treatment there was all about repetitive action and building the neural pathways between the brain and the muscles. The idea was that Nic could train his brain to understand and therefore do certain things. It was never going to be a miracle, but it did improve his balance and, while there, we started to discuss Nic having a tendon-release operation early. The original doctors had told us that it would be best to wait until Nic had stopped growing, but this consultant thought it would be possible to do it sooner and that it would really help Nic's specific case. By the age of four, he couldn't open his legs, his knees were totally bent and he was entirely on his tiptoes. He used to walk with a frame, but it was very difficult. He had to wear these big boots to keep his ankles straight and any kind of movement was really awkward for him.

In the end, we decided to go ahead and Nic had the release operation in his groin, the backs of his knees and the backs of his ankles. He was in plaster from his groin to his toes with both legs, of course; I stayed overnight in the hospital with him (and carried him out of bed into a wheelchair, as that was just what was expected of you). When we finally got him home, he slept for 24 hours and that was that. The very next day, still in his little frame, he *stood up* on his plasters. He was incredible, actually; he was just always an incredible child. Nic was always the joker, always comical even as a kid, and used his humour and good nature to make friends with everyone. After he had his operation, he was in plaster for about six weeks and then he was just off, bombing around in his frame, rolling over and making everyone laugh. After a lot of intense physio, his legs were straight and his feet could touch the floor, so then, at four years old, he had to learn to walk. As he got older, his muscles became tighter again, which is why the physio and stretching had to become a part of his life, as you can't just keep operating and lengthening tendons indefinitely.

Nic did so well with walking, and he used to play football after school too. He couldn't kick the ball, but he would run around and love it. He went on to play for Stevenage football team and got man of the match many times, because he was so determined and enthusiastic. I was so happy for him, so happy to see how happy it made him. Generally, I was too busy to really think about anything we were missing out on as a family. Racing takes over your life. It wasn't like a hobby; it was all-consuming for all of us. To be fair, I wasn't the mother-and-toddler-group kind of person anyway, so I wouldn't have been going to things like that even if Nic had been able-bodied and we hadn't been moving around so much. However, he did have birthday parties at bowling and the softplay, and he would always mix in. He'd be climbing up the ladder to get to the top and then screeching down the slide. He never just sat at the edge watching other kids.

I wasn't a hard mum, in the sense that I love Nic immensely and he has always, always known that. I would do *anything* for him. But I always tried to make him do things himself and challenged him to stretch himself because I knew he could do it. I was brought up as a dad's girl. I was very rough and tumble and my dad treated me like a boy. My sister wasn't as tomboyish, she was more your traditional girl, whereas I was never scared of falling, tripping or getting a few scrapes and bruises. Nic used to fall over regularly when he was young, and he still does occasionally today. If I was in the supermarket, people would rush over and I'd say, please leave him. I think people thought I was this awful, horrible mother, but my instinct was to not scare him. I didn't want him to be afraid of falling because I knew it was going to be an inevitable part of his life. I didn't want him to think his mum was scared of him falling or even that falling was frightening. I wanted him to bounce back as second nature and start to build the resilience I knew that he would need. Of course, if Nic were really going to hurt himself, there was no question of me letting that happen, but all children get scrapes and bruises, and I didn't want him to feel scared of that just because he had a disability.

There is a lot of judgement about the way disabled children are raised. I mean, people love to judge about any kind of parenting, but there is a particular focus when your child has a visible disability. I'm lucky in that I've never been worried about what other people think. If I don't know them, they don't know me, so they can't judge me, because they don't know the ins and outs. If a member of my family said something about a parenting choice, I would explain why we were doing things the way we were. For example, I used to strap Nic's feet to his bike pedals with Velcro (the bike had stabilizers) and my mum would be worried sick. We would go out on bike rides, the three of us together, and Mum would be saying, 'Oh Linda, I don't know about this.' But my outlook was always, what was the real risk? If he was wearing a helmet and he fell, the worst that could happen was that he might scrape his hands. Which is exactly the same as any other kid.

I understand why people are so protective of disabled children – this is another instinct, because you know they are additionally vulnerable. You can't change that way of thinking for a lot of people and there will be those who say, 'I could never do that to my child.' But I always saw the risk of saying, 'That's not for you', the risk of saying, 'No, you can't have fun like other boys', as worse. I didn't want to stop him doing things, I didn't want him to miss out on anything that able-bodied children did, and I really felt, instinctually, that making a plan so he could join in would help him in the future.

As Nic grew, he wanted to do everything for himself. There were some things which, of course, he would need help with – that was just automatic for us. But he never complained once about his condition and never asked for help. He just went ahead and tried to make a plan. If you were to say to Nic, 'You can't do that', he'd say, '*Can't?* I can do anything if I try.' *Can't* just isn't in Nic's vocabulary. I do think we planted that seed very young, although I hadn't really realized what I was doing. I'm sure there were moments when it gave me heartache not to help him when I could have made things easier for him, but it was always about what was best for him. I knew that, when he was older, he wouldn't want to be reliant on other people: he would want to do things for himself. The thing with Nic is that, even to this day, he never gets embarrassed. If he falls up a step, he doesn't care. It's not nice to see for me, you know, it breaks my heart. But he doesn't think anything of it. He just gets up and off he goes again. He still bounces to this day.

When Nic first said he wanted to race, my initial reaction was *no*. Not again. Please don't. I still say it to him now! At the beginning, I was like, what on earth are we doing here? Why is he even in this car? Then there was the crash at Thruxton, and I cried my eyes out. I'd kept it together on the day of the crash itself, but the next day I read a headline in the paper saying, 'Nicolas

Hamilton in Near-Fatal Crash' and I just collapsed. I was on my own and I thought, I can't let him do this, he needs to get out of the car. It just broke me. But Nic being Nic was having none of it. 'Mum, it will be fine, it will never happen again.' And you actually can't stop them from doing it. I can't physically stop him. So, you have to accept that they are going to take their own risks. Look, it's still difficult. It's still difficult with Lewis. I worry myself into an early grave about both of them – they're both driving over 100mph around a circuit. While it's true it's one of the safest sports out there, it is still dangerous and, of course, there is the chance that they could get seriously hurt. That worry is something I have to try to manage, but I've never been able to get over it.

When Nic had some of his down times from racing, it was very hard, although he rarely shared his low moments. I never knew anything about the bullying at school and, even though we are very close and speak for hours, he has always kept certain things back. During the hard times in racing, I felt dreadful for him but, you see, Anthony didn't. Because he was like, he's out there driving the car like everyone else, struggling to get sponsorship like everyone else, treat him like everyone else. If he needs special treatment, he shouldn't be in the car in the first place. He gave him no leeway whatsoever. Anthony only does everything for the best for his boys and he will be harsh with Nic in the same way he was with Lewis, simply because it pushes them to be better. Anthony can sometimes be the pusher, whereas I'm the catcher, trying to explain it in a different way – you'll be fine, just keep going. Today, both of the boys are such incredibly hard workers, and they now do all that pushing themselves. People don't realize how hard Lewis works – and has worked since he was eight years old. He is one of the hardest working Formula 1 drivers and you'll often still find him at the circuit at 11 at night. And Nic is the same. He will push and push himself and never be satisfied. It's always, no, I can do better.

What Nic has achieved is incredible. Beyond the racing, he is an incredible human being. He just has this way about him that draws people in. When he was younger, he spent a lot of time in the company of adults. We were always away racing and, as Lewis is seven years older than Nic, he was also most often with the older boys, aside from some of their younger siblings whom Nic would play with. Or else he was with adults. At ten years old he could hold an adult conversation and that maturity has stayed with him. He is also *so* determined. The most determined person that I have ever met.

I do think it is important to say that you've got to work with what you've got, and everybody is different. As the parent of any child, if you are going to wrap them up in cotton wool, they are going to be in cotton wool for the rest of their lives and will expect to be helped, will even need to be helped at every avenue. Whereas if you don't, they have to find a way. Nic, you can get down yourself. I can't keep carrying you. Nic, you can eat this yourself, try again. And then eventually, as they get older, they find their own way.

We never spoke about mental health in our day, but watching the way Nic connects with people through their emotional struggles has been amazing. Look, he's my son, so it's difficult for me to have perspective, but I can see objectively that he is an extraordinary and inspirational person. He is just so strong and driven and has this determination that gets him through everything. He does something to everyone he meets simply through the way he is, the way he talks or the way he makes them feel. There is almost no stopping him, even though it is still so difficult for him. It breaks my heart knowing that he is in pain every day. If I could give him my legs, I would. In a heartbeat. But I just can't. There is actually nothing that I can change about his condition.

If we had wrapped him in cotton wool, Nic would probably still be living at home and I'd be bringing his food for him and helping him eat. I remember, and this is so silly looking back, but my biggest worry when he went to secondary school was that I thought he'd never be able to tie his shoelaces. There are certain things that just get you and I was really concerned that someone might have to help him or pick on him about it. 'Can't even do his shoelaces.' I didn't want him to feel he couldn't get himself ready for school any more, so he was going to have to learn. So, we sat and sat, and we practised and practised, until he got there and did his own shoelaces. While we have always accepted his condition, we never accepted that the limits were set in stone.

I'm so proud of you, Nic. It's a big word. We get it a lot, Anthony and me. 'You must be so proud of the boys,' everyone says. So, for me to say I'm very proud does feel a bit obvious. But I am in awe of you, Nic. I'm in awe of what you have achieved. You have achieved the almost unachievable. Watching you go from where you started as this tiny little baby who came too soon into the world, to where you are today, is just beyond impressive. And you have achieved it all by yourself – no matter what you say, no one else has made this happen. You are a total inspiration to so many people, to adults as well as children, I don't think you realize the extent of your impact. You inspire me, you inspire Lewis, you inspire your dad. You inspire everybody. You are just a very special person, and I am so proud to be your mum.

ENDNOTES

1. National Institue of Economic & Social Research, 'The Fiscal Costs and Benefits of Problem Gambling: Towards Better Estimates', 14 April 2023, pp. 4 and 23, https://www.niesr.ac.uk/wp-content/uploads/2023/04/The-Fiscal-Costs-and-Benefits-of-Problem-Gambling.pdf
2. Public Health England/ Office for Health Improvement & Disparities, 'Gambling Related Harms Evidence Review: Summary', Gov.uk, updated January 2023, 3.1, https://www.gov.uk/government/publications/gambling-related-harms-evidence-review/gambling-related-harms-evidence-review-summary--2
3. YouGov, 'Annual GB Treatment and Support Survey 2022', commissioned by the charity GambleAware, 2022, p. 6, https://www.begambleaware.org/sites/default/files/2023-07/GambleAware%20Treatment%20and%20Support%20Report%20July%202022.pdf
4. Grall-Bronnec, M., et al., 'Gambling among European Professional Athletes. Prevalence and Associated Factors', J Addict Dis, Oct–Dec 2016, 35 (4): 278–290. doi: 10.1080/10550887.2016.1177807. https://pubmed.ncbi.nlm.nih.gov/27111296/
5. Office for National Statistics (ONS), 'Suicides in England and Wales: 2021 Registrations', 6 September 2022, statistical bulletin, https://www.ons.gov.

uk/peoplepopulationandcommunity/birthsdeathsandmarriages/deaths/bulletins/suicidesintheunitedkingdom/2021registrations

6. Department of Health and Social Care and The Rt Hon Sajid Javid MP, 'Men Urged to Talk about Mental Health to Prevent Suicide', gov.uk, 24 June 2022, https://www.gov.uk/government/news/men-urged-to-talk-about-mental-health-to-prevent-suicide
7. Priory Group, 1000 respondents, 'Men's Mental Health: 40% of Men Won't Talk about Their Mental Health', https://www.priorygroup.com/blog/40-of-men-wont-talk-to-anyone-about-their-mental-health

RESOURCES

Having read my story and about some of the issues I have faced, you might find yourself wanting to delve deeper into areas that relate to your own personal story or problems you're having. So here are some resources that might be helpful to you.

Mind

A charity offering information about mental health, as well as practical and therapeutic support.
www.mind.org.uk

Samaritans

A 24-hour listening service, providing emotional support in person, online and on the phone for those feeling lonely or distressed.
www.samaritans.co.uk

CALM (Campaign Against Living Miserably)

CALM's helpline and livechat are open from 5pm to midnight every day, 365 days a year.
www.thecalmzone.net/get-support

GambleAware

Free, confidential help and support to anyone who's worried about their – or someone else's – gambling.
www.begambleaware.org

ACKNOWLEDGEMENTS

Although this book is mostly about me, my journey, my story and how I have gone through my life. Behind every great man is a mountain of great people. Each and every person I have met and encountered in my life, both positive or negative, has been a huge part of my journey to self-acceptance and growth. It is impossible for me to call-out each and every one of my friends to show my gratitude for their continued support and efforts to make me feel welcomed in their world. YOU ALL KNOW, WHO YOU ARE and without you all, I would not be the strong character I am today. All of you have impacted me hugely in your own way, taught me, inspired me and accepted me as me. This book mentions the huge gratitude and impact my family have on my life, however, I would have not been able to have written this book without my incredible friends either. This book is for you all and I hope you find some sort of satisfaction for being a part of my life, somewhere in these pages. This is your book too.

ABOUT THE AUTHOR

Nicolas Hamilton is a British racing driver who currently competes in the British Touring Car Championship.

Alongside Nicolas's racing career, he is a prolific public speaker and uses his social media platform to reach beyond fans of motorsport. He has been featured in British Vogue and worked with a variety of brands such as Meta, Amazon, and MINI to name a few, sharing his clear vision and understanding of how brands can improve diverse representation.

Now That I Have Your Attention is his first book.